Texts *for* English Language Development

BENCHMARK EDUCATION COMPANY

Table of Contents

Essential Question

How can government influence the way we live?

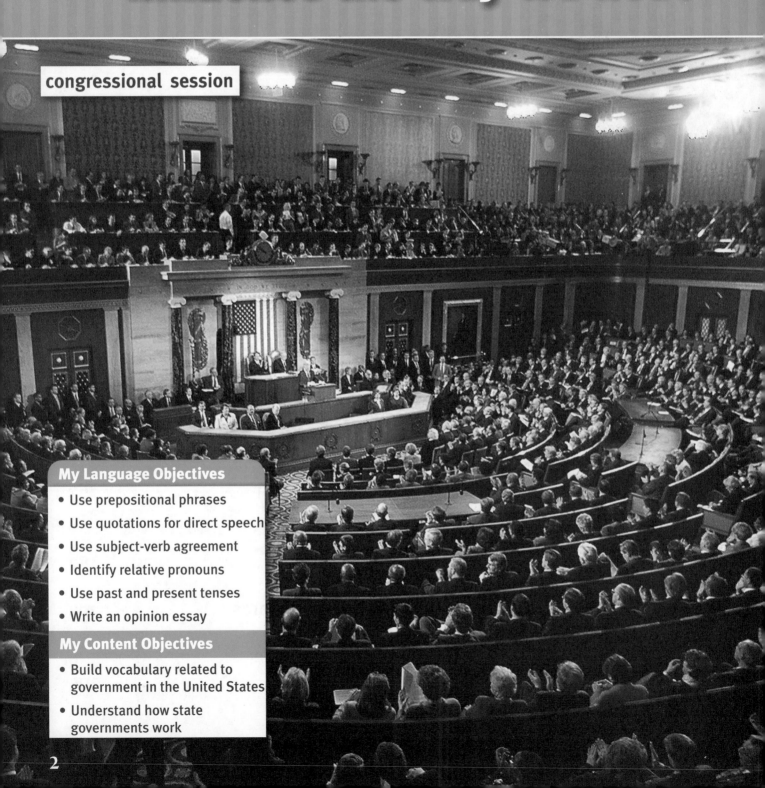

congressional session

My Language Objectives

- Use prepositional phrases
- Use quotations for direct speech
- Use subject-verb agreement
- Identify relative pronouns
- Use past and present tenses
- Write an opinion essay

My Content Objectives

- Build vocabulary related to government in the United States
- Understand how state governments work

emergency fire truck

rescue worker

3

Solving Problems by Lisa Benjamin

1

In the United States...federal, state, and local governments often work as a team to solve problems.

2

For example, after an earthquake or floods...people might need food or shelter....

3

In recent years the shellfish population of Washington State has declined due to pollution in Puget Sound....

4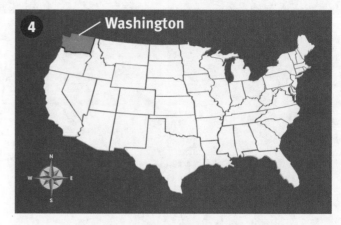

Washington

To protect Washington's resources, the state and federal government joined together to form the Washington Shellfish Initiative.

1. ThinkSpeakListen

Describe an example from "Solving Problems" that shows how government helps people in the United States.

Use Prepositional Phrases

Where?

In the United States…federal, state, and local governments often work as a team to solve problems.

When?

For example, **after an earthquake or floods**…people might need food or shelter.

When?

In recent years the shellfish population of Washington State has declined due to pollution in Puget Sound.

Who or What?

Washington's aquaculture industry contributes more than $270 million **to the state economy**.

2. ThinkSpeakListen

Why do writers use examples to support their statements?

The First Town Meeting
An excerpt from *The People of Sparks*

by Jeanne DuPrau

The story takes place in the future. Only a few people still survive on Earth. They live in small settlements, or towns. Mary, Ben, and Wilmer are leaders in one of the towns, called Sparks.

Mary, Ben, and Wilmer have a problem. Some people have come from another town. They need food and shelter, but Sparks does not have much to share. What will they do?

 "They can't stay here. There are too many of them. Where would we put them? How would we feed them?"

 "They could go up to Pine Gap. Maybe."

 "Don't be ridiculous. That's at least two weeks' walk away. How could these feeble people travel that far? How could they carry enough food with them?"

Ben and Wilmer are quiet. They know Mary is right.

 "So what do we do, if they can't stay and they can't go? What is the right thing to do?"

 "Well, there's the Pioneer.[1] As a temporary solution."

 "True."

 "A good thought.... We'll give them water and food. ... In exchange,...they help in the fields.... After a while, when they're stronger...they can set up their own village somewhere else."

1. Pioneer—a hotel in the town

3. ThinkSpeakListen

What do you think of the townspeople's "temporary solution" for the people of Sparks?

Saving Yellowstone

Each year, over three million people visit Yellowstone National Park.... They hike its trails and swim in its lakes and rivers....

Yellowstone has an important role in American history as the nation's first national park. In 1871, Ferdinand Hayden led a group of explorers into the Yellowstone River Basin.... He convinced lawmakers that Yellowstone should remain in its natural state. They agreed and passed a bill to protect the area and establish a national park....

Ferdinand Hayden

At first, volunteers took care of the park.... Today, park rangers and other staff members maintain the park.

4. ThinkSpeakListen

Explain why Yellowstone National Park has an important role in history.

Use Quotations for Direct Speech

"They can't stay here. There are too many of them. How would we feed them?"

"They could go up to Pine Gap. Maybe."

"Don't be ridiculous. How could they carry enough food with them?"

"Well, there's the Pioneer. As a temporary solution."

5. ThinkSpeakListen

What do you think the people of Sparks will do next?

The State Government and Its Citizens

by Lisa Simone

The Three Branches of State Government

The state's **legislative branch** writes new laws and makes amendments, or changes, to old laws. This branch includes representatives and senators who are elected by voters....

The state's **executive branch** carries out the laws passed by legislators. In state government, the governor, who is elected by popular vote, leads this branch....

Finally, the **judicial branch** includes judges who interpret the laws of a state. In some states, voters elect judges. In other states, the governor appoints judges....

What Does the State Government Do?

④

1. State governments run hospitals to care for sick people.

2. They also monitor the grounds of parks and other public spaces owned by the state.

3. State police patrol the highways to keep people safe.

The state government...protects the health and safety of its citizens.

⑤

1. They work with cities and towns to set up school districts, which are run by local school boards.

2. The state government gives school boards some of the money they need to hire teachers and purchase books and other materials.

3. Most state governments fund about 50 percent of the money needed to run public schools.

State governments are responsible for educating their citizens, too.

6. ThinkSpeakListen

Summarize how state governments protect the health and safety of their citizens.

The Role of the Governor

The governor sets a budget to decide how the state's money should be spent....

A governor often attends important state events and ceremonies.

She or he works to attract new businesses to the state by meeting with leaders from other states or countries.

The governor also appoints officials to state agencies that work to improve life for the people of the state.

7. ThinkSpeakListen

Describe the role of a state governor.

Use Subject-Verb Agreement

Subject	Verb
Each state	is responsible for protecting "the lives and liberties" of its own citizens.
Also, different states	have different issues.
For instance, water conservation	is a big issue in California because of the severe drought there.
Each state government	responds to the specific needs of its citizens.

8. ThinkSpeakListen

How does the government in your state help its citizens?

Fifty States Plus

The United States includes a number of regions that aren't actual states. The people there are full citizens, but they have different relationships with the nation's government.

For example, the nation's capital, Washington, District of Columbia (D.C.), is a federal district governed by Congress.... Residents of Washington, D.C., have one elected representative in Congress but no senators.

Another home to U.S. citizens that is not a state is the Commonwealth of Puerto Rico.... In addition to Puerto Rico, four other locations classified as territories are home to U.S. citizens. They are Guam, American Samoa, the Virgin Islands, and the Northern Mariana Islands. The federal government also oversees a number of uninhabited islands. Most of these are in the Pacific Ocean.

9. ThinkSpeakListen

Explain how Washington, D.C., is different from a state government.

Identify Relative Pronouns

	Noun	Relative Pronoun	
	The governor also appoints officials to <u>state agencies</u>	<u>that</u>	work to improve life for the people of the state.
	Finally, the judicial branch includes <u>judges</u>	<u>who</u>	interpret the laws of a state.
	They work with cities and towns to set up <u>school districts</u>,	<u>which</u>	are run by local school boards.

10. ThinkSpeakListen

Summarize the main ideas in "Fifty States Plus."

Stanley's Release

An excerpt from *Holes* by Louis Sachar

In *Holes*, 15-year-old Stanley Yelnats has been sent to a detention center for a crime he did not commit. Every day Stanley and the other boys at the center have to dig holes that are five feet deep. The Texas Attorney General (A.G.), who is the law enforcement chief, comes to the camp with Stanley's lawyer, Ms. Morengo, to demand his release.

(1) *In this scene, the Attorney General and Ms. Morengo come back to the camp office from the field where Stanley has been digging holes. Stanley holds a suitcase he found while digging. It is a suitcase full of jewels.*

They slowly walked back to camp. The tall man was the Texas Attorney General, the chief law enforcement officer for the state. Stanley's lawyer was named Ms. Morengo.

Stanley held the suitcase. He was so tired he couldn't think straight....

They stopped in front of the camp office. Mr. Sir went inside to get Stanley's belongings....

Ms. Morengo put a hand on Stanley's shoulder and told him to hang in there. He would be seeing his parents soon.

(2) *The Warden is the director of the camp. She knows there is something valuable in the suitcase. She orders Stanley to open it.*

Hector Zeroni (Zero) is Stanley's best friend.

Mr. Pendanski and Mr. Sir work at the camp.

"He has not been officially released," said the Warden. "Open the suitcase, Stanley!"

"Do not open it," said Stanley's lawyer.

Stanley did nothing....

The Attorney General handed Ms. Morengo a sheet of paper. "You're free to go," he said to Stanley....

Stanley stopped and turned to look at Zero. He couldn't just leave him here.

Zero gave him thumbs-up.

"I can't leave Hector," Stanley said.

"I suggest we go," said his lawyer with a sense of urgency in her voice.

"I'll be okay," said Zero. His eyes shifted toward Mr. Pendanski on one side of him, then to the Warden and Mr. Sir on the other.

"There's nothing I can do for your friend," said Ms. Morengo. "You are released pursuant to an order from the judge."

"They'll kill him," said Stanley.

"Your friend is not in danger," said the Attorney General. "There's going to be an investigation into everything that's happened here. For the present, I am taking charge of the camp."

11. ThinkSpeakListen

How is Stanley feeling in this part of the story? Why do you think so?

(3) *The Attorney General tells the Warden to find the computer file with information about Zero. Mr. Pendanski says that Zero's file is missing.*

The Attorney General's office also cannot find information about Zero in its records.

"My office is having some difficulty locating Hector Zeroni's records," the Attorney General said.

"So you have no claim of authority over him?" asked Ms. Morengo.

"I didn't say that. He's in the computer. We just can't access his records. It's like they've fallen through a hole in cyberspace."...

"So what are you planning to do with him?"...

The Attorney General stared at her. "He was obviously incarcerated for a reason."

"Oh? And what reason was that?"

The Attorney General said nothing.

Stanley's lawyer took hold of Zero's hand. "C'mon, Hector, you're coming with us."

12. ThinkSpeakListen

How might Stanley's feelings have changed as this part of the story comes to an end? Why do you think so?

Use Past and Present Tenses

Verb	Present Tenses	Past Tenses
Wait	I wait I am waiting	I waited I was waiting
Talk	I talk I am talking	I talked I was talking
Stop	I stop I am stopping	I stopped I was stopping

13. ThinkSpeakListen

Describe something you are doing now (in the present). Then describe something you did yesterday (in the past).

Go, Botoño!

Zoey Botoño looked up through the dome of Primaluna. From her yard on the lunar colony, Earth looked like a blue-white beach ball floating in the cosmos....

Four months ago, Primaluna had become an official territory of the United States. Now the colony was about to elect its first governor....

If she became governor, the whole family could travel there for official occasions. How would they feel about such an enormous change in lifestyle?...

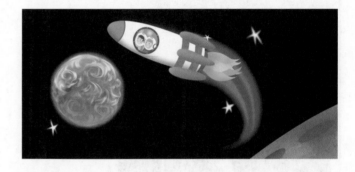

A glass bowl sat on the table, full of folded votes. She opened them one at a time.... She called her family into the kitchen. "You've made your voices heard," she said. "You've told me it's okay to run for governor."...

14. ThinkSpeakListen

As a territory, what kind of government will Primaluna have?

Writing to Sources

Do you think the government portrayed in "Stanley's Release" does a good job of protecting its citizens? Write an opinion essay in which you answer this question, using details and evidence from "Stanley's Release."

Question You Will Answer

Genre You Will Write In

Sources You Will Use

Sample Essay

The government does a good job of protecting the rights of its citizens in "Stanley's Release." The character of the Attorney General is a representative of the state government. He acts to protect the boys at the detention center who have been treated cruelly and unfairly.

Introduction:
Introduce your topic.

State your opinion.

First, the Attorney General comes to the camp with an order from a state judge to release Stanley Yelnats. Stanley is being punished for a crime he did not commit. The Attorney General arrives at the camp with Stanley's lawyer and the judge's order to release Stanley to his parents. Stanley's rights have been violated, and the Attorney General protects those rights.

Main idea 1:
State main idea of paragraph.

Support main idea with evidence.

Also, while the Attorney General is at Camp Green Lake, he sees that the other boys at the camp need legal protection. Each day the boys must dig holes that are five feet deep and five feet wide. This is very hard work, even for adults. The boys' rights as citizens are violated. For this reason, Stanley does not want to leave Hector Zeroni behind, but the Attorney General assures Stanley that Hector will be okay. The Attorney General takes over as head of the camp. He says, "There's going to be an investigation into everything that's happened here.... I am taking charge of the camp."

Main idea 2:
State main idea of paragraph.

Support main idea with evidence.

The Texas Attorney General first makes certain Stanley is released. He then lets Hector go with Stanley's lawyer. Finally, he takes charge of the detention center to make sure all the boys there will be treated fairly and according to the law. By taking these actions, he very successfully protects their rights as U.S. citizens.

Conclusion:
Restate opinion and conclude essay.

Essential Question

How do we reveal ourselves to others?

Dorothy, the Tin Man, and the Scarecrow

My Language Objectives

- Use adjectives to signal states of being
- Describe with similes
- Connect events by combining clauses
- Use modal auxiliaries
- Use adverbials to add detail
- Write an informative essay

My Content Objectives

- Build vocabulary related to personal states of being
- Understand different ways in which we reveal ourselves to others

Peter Pan

the huntsman and the boar

23

The Gnat and the Lion

by Aesop

1

"Away with you, vile insect!" said a lion angrily to a gnat that buzzed around its head....

The next instant, the gnat flew at the lion and stung him sharply on the nose....

2

The proud gnat buzzed away to tell the whole world about his victory. But instead he flew straight into a spider's web.

And there, he who had defeated the king of beasts came to a miserable end—the prey of a little spider.

1. ThinkSpeakListen

Recount in your own words one key event in the story.

Use Adjectives to Signal States of Being

meaning:

disgusting or very annoying

synonyms:

horrible, nasty, aggravating, irritating

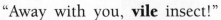

"Away with you, **vile** insect!"

I made sure to stay away from the vile sewer water.

The **proud** gnat buzzed away to tell the whole world about his victory.

And there, he who had defeated the king of beasts came to a **miserable** end.

2. ThinkSpeakListen

Use adjectives to describe the characters from "The Gnat and the Lion."

Snow White Meets the Huntsman

An excerpt from *Snow White and the Seven Dwarfs*

by the Brothers Grimm

Once upon a time in midwinter, when the snowflakes were falling like feathers from heaven, a queen sat sewing at her window.... She thought to herself, "If only I had a child as white as snow...."

Soon afterward the queen had a little daughter who was as white as snow...Therefore they called her Little Snow White. Sadly, as soon as the child was born, the queen died.

A year later the king took himself another wife. She was a beautiful woman, but she was proud and arrogant. She could not stand it if anyone might surpass her in beauty....

Snow White grew up and became.... as beautiful as the light of day, even more beautiful than the queen herself....

The queen took fright and turned yellow and green with envy.

3. ThinkSpeakListen

Describe what happens in this story.

Melamut the Crocodile

Melamut the crocodile was the most ferocious creature in the Nile River; indeed, in all of Egypt.... Surprisingly, there was something that made Melamut tremble. She was terrified of the dentist. For a crocodile with sixty-six teeth, that was an *enormous* problem.

One day, Melamut was lying on the riverbank with her mouth wide open. A small gray-and-black bird called a plover perched on Melamut...The plover had a proposition. "I'll clean your teeth—and get a delicious meal, too—but you must keep your mouth open wide. I don't intend to be a crocodile appetizer."

Melamut agreed, so the bird hopped inside the huge jaws and removed every bit of food stuck between Melamut's teeth. They sparkled!

4. ThinkSpeakListen

How does the cooperation of Melamut and the plover benefit both of them?

Describe with Similes

Soon afterward the queen had a little daughter who was **as white as snow**…Therefore they called her Little Snow White.

…daughter… ⟶ **…as white as snow**…

Snow White grew up and became…**as beautiful as the light of day,** even more beautiful than the queen herself.

Snow White… ⟶ **…as beautiful as the light of day**…

5. ThinkSpeakListen

Create similes using words from "Melamut the Crocodile."

Come Away, Come Away!

An excerpt from the novel *Peter and Wendy*

by J. M. Barrie

1 There was another light in the room now…It was a fairy, no longer than your hand, but still growing. It was a girl called Tinker Bell.…

2 A moment after the fairy's entrance the window was blown open by the breathing of the little stars, and Peter dropped in.…

3 "Tinker Bell," he called softly…"Tell me, do you know where they put my shadow?"…

4 Tink said that the shadow was in the big box. She meant the chest of drawers, and Peter jumped at the drawers…In a moment he had recovered his shadow…

6. ThinkSpeakListen

What do you think Peter is going to do next?

If he thought at all…it was that he and his shadow, when brought near each other, would join like drops of water, and when they did not he was appalled.

He tried to stick it on with soap from the bathroom, but that also failed…and he sat on the floor and cried.

His sobs woke Wendy, and she sat up in bed….

"Boy," she said courteously, "why are you crying?"…

"I can't get my shadow to stick on…."

Then Wendy saw the shadow on the floor, looking so draggled, and she was frightfully sorry for Peter....

Fortunately she knew at once what to do. "It must be sewn on," she said, just a little patronizingly.... She got out her sewing bag and sewed the shadow onto Peter's foot....

"Perhaps I should have ironed it," Wendy said thoughtfully, but Peter, boylike, was indifferent to appearances, and he was now jumping about in the wildest glee.

7. ThinkSpeakListen

Describe Peter Pan's personality and Wendy's personality.

Connect Events by Combining Clauses

Event	Connecting Word	Event
...the window was blown open by the breathing of the little stars,	**and**	Peter dropped in.

Event	Connecting Word	Event
He tried to stick it on with soap from the bathroom,	**but**	that also failed.

Event	Connecting Word	Event
Then Wendy saw the shadow on the floor, looking so draggled,	**and**	she was frightfully sorry for Peter.

8. ThinkSpeakListen

Explain why a writer might want to combine clauses to connect events.

Peter, the Wild Boy

Some writers have suggested that James Matthew Barrie based the character Peter Pan in part on an actual boy. In 1725, a boy was discovered living wild in a forest in Germany. He appeared to be around twelve years old, walked on all fours, and climbed trees.... He could not communicate and was frightened by people....

Peter the Wild Boy

The boy captured the interest of England's royal family. They named him Peter. King George I took Peter to live in London with his daughter-in-law, Princess Caroline, who took over Peter's care and education....

King George I

Princess Caroline realized Peter would probably be happier in the countryside, so she sent him to live on a farm. He remained there until he died. He was around seventy years old.

Princess Caroline

9. ThinkSpeakListen

How do you think Peter the Wild Boy came to live alone in the forest?

Writing to Sources

According to the narrator of "Come Away, Come Away!," "there never was a cockier boy" than Peter Pan. What story details support this view of Peter's character? Write an informative essay in which you answer this question, using details and evidence from "Come Away, Come Away!"

Question

Type of Writing

Purpose for Writing

Sources You Will Use

Sample Essay

In "Come Away, Come Away!," the narrator states that "there never was a cockier boy" than Peter Pan. In Peter's interactions with Wendy, we see him show this cockiness. First, he refuses to admit that he is sad. Then, when Wendy helps him, he takes credit for something that she has done.

When Wendy wakes up, she hears Peter crying because he can't reattach his shadow. She asks him many questions to learn about him, and when she hears that Peter has no mother, she says, "O Peter, no wonder you were crying." Peter, however, claims that he wasn't crying. He is too proud to admit that his feelings can be hurt by anything.

Later, after Wendy has helped Peter to reattach his shadow, Peter jumps up and shouts about how clever he is. He is very proud of himself, and forgets what Wendy has done for him. Peter is so cocky that he cannot admit, or even remember, that he needs the help of others.

As a result of Peter's cockiness, he is unable to admit that he is weak in any way. He will not confess to Wendy that his feelings have been hurt, and he will not acknowledge that he has needed her help. However, in the end, he does show that he is not completely self-absorbed, when he admits to Wendy that "one girl is more use than twenty boys."

The introduction lets the reader know the topic of the essay. The writer uses the words "first" and "then" to summarize events in order.

The body paragraphs give details that support the main idea of the essay: Peter's cockiness. The writer uses adjectives to describe Peter's personality and state of mind.

The conclusion summarizes the main points of the essay and provides a closing statement that tells us something else about Peter's pride.

How Dorothy Saved the Scarecrow

An excerpt from
The Wonderful Wizard of Oz

by L. Frank Baum

Dorothy bade her friends good-bye, and again started along the road of yellow brick. When she had gone several miles she thought she would stop to rest, and so climbed to the top of the fence beside the road and sat down…Not far away she saw a Scarecrow, placed high on a pole… Its head was a small sack stuffed with straw, with eyes, nose, and mouth painted on it to represent a face….

While Dorothy was looking earnestly into the odd, painted face of the Scarecrow, she was surprised to see one of the eyes slowly wink at her…. She climbed down from the fence and walked up to it, while Toto ran around the pole and barked.

10. ThinkSpeakListen
In your opinion, why is Toto running around the pole and barking? Why do you think so?

3

"Good day," said the Scarecrow, in a rather husky voice.... "How do you do?"

"I'm pretty well, thank you," replied Dorothy politely. "How do you do?"

"I'm not feeling well," said the Scarecrow, with a smile…"This pole is stuck up my back. If you will please take away the pole I shall be greatly obliged to you."

Dorothy reached up both arms and lifted the figure off the pole…

4

"Who are you?" asked the Scarecrow when he had stretched himself and yawned. "And where are you going?"

"My name is Dorothy," said the girl, "and I am going to the Emerald City, to ask the Great Oz to send me back to Kansas."…

5 "Do you think," he asked, "if I go to the Emerald City with you, that Oz would give me some brains?"

"I cannot tell," she returned, "but you may come with me, if you like.... I'll ask Oz to do all he can for you."

"Thank you," he answered gratefully.

They walked back to the road. Dorothy helped him over the fence, and they started along the path of yellow brick for the Emerald City.

11. ThinkSpeakListen
Describe Dorothy's personality and the Scarecrow's personality.

Use Adverbials to Add Detail

While Dorothy was looking **earnestly** into the odd, painted face of the Scarecrow…

"Good day," said the Scarecrow, **in a rather husky voice**…. "How do you do?"

"I cannot tell," she returned, "but you may come with me, if you like…. I'll ask Oz to do all he can **for you**."

12. ThinkSpeakListen

Describe some of the events of "How Dorothy Saved the Scarecrow" using adverbials to add detail.

The Wonderful World of Oz

L. Frank Baum wrote fifteen books about the fantasyland called Oz. The first book in the series is *The Wonderful Wizard of Oz*. In this story, a Kansas farm girl named Dorothy Gale and her dog, Toto, are blown away in a tornado. They land in Oz. There they have many adventures…

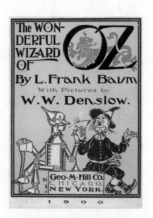

The Marvelous Land of Oz is the first sequel. This tale revolves around the adventures of a new character—a boy named Tip who escapes from a wicked sorceress and travels to the Emerald City to begin a new life.…

In the third book in the series, *Ozma of Oz*…Dorothy is washed overboard on a voyage to Australia and lands on an enchanted island where she meets Princess Ozma. The two join forces as they try to free the island's imprisoned queen and her children.

13. ThinkSpeakListen
In what ways are *The Marvelous Land of Oz* and *Ozma of Oz* different from "How Dorothy Saved the Scarecrow"?

Use Modal Auxiliaries

"Do you think," he asked, "if I go to the Emerald City with you, that Oz **would** give me some brains?"

"I **cannot** tell," she returned...

"...but you **may** come with me, if you like..."

"...I'll ask Oz to do all he **can** for you."

14. ThinkSpeakListen

Discuss what you might ask of the Great Oz if you were to visit him. Use these words in your conversation: **would, cannot, can, may.**

Essential Question

How do we respond to nature?

nature writer John Burroughs

My Language Objectives

- Use prepositional phrases about place
- Add detail with adjectives
- Use transition words and phrases to connect events
- Use commas
- Understand words using context clues
- Build research skills

My Content Objectives

- Build vocabulary related to observation of the natural world
- Understand how human beings observe and respond to nature

chipmunk on a tree trunk

young boy enjoying nature

43

A Bird's Free Lunch

an excerpt from *The Wit of a Duck and Other Papers*

by John Burroughs

John Burroughs was an author who wrote essays about nature. He especially enjoyed writing about birds and flowers.

One winter, I fastened pieces of suet…upon the tree in front of my window. Then, I sat at my desk and watched the birds eat their free lunch.

The jays bossed the woodpeckers. The woodpeckers bossed the chickadees. And the chickadees bossed the kinglet….

None of the birds will eat lean meat. They want the clear fat. The jays alight upon it and peck away with great vigor, almost standing on tiptoe to get the proper sweep.

The woodpecker uses his head alone in pecking, but the jay's action involves the whole body. Yet his blows are softer, not so sharp and abrupt as those of the woodpecker.

1. ThinkSpeakListen

What are the differences between the way the woodpecker and the blue jay peck at the food on the tree?

Use Prepositional Phrases about Place

Subject + Verb: *Who* is doing *what*?	Preposition + Object = Prepositional Phrase: *Where*?
One winter, I fastened pieces of suet…	upon the tree…
Then, I sat	at my desk and watched the birds eat their free lunch.
The kinglet…became quite tame, and one day alighted…	upon my arm as I stood leaning against the tree.
I fancied him	in one of my thick spruces, his head under his tiny wing,…

2. ThinkSpeakListen

What are some of the locations to which prepositions can point?

The Shimerdas
an excerpt from *My Ántonia* by Willa Cather

Willa Cather

In this excerpt from My Ántonia, *the name of the narrator is Jim Burden. He is telling the story of his life as a boy. When his parents died, he moved from Virginia to live with his grandparents on the Nebraska prairie. His neighbors were the Shimerdas.*

While grandmother took the pitchfork...and dug potatoes, I picked them up out of the soft brown earth and put them into the bag...looking up at the hawks....

When grandmother was ready to go, I said I would like to stay.... She peered down at me..."Aren't you afraid of snakes?" "A little," I admitted, "but I like to stay..."

"Well, if you see one, don't have anything to do with him. The big yellow and brown ones won't hurt you; they're bull-snakes and help to keep the gophers down.

"Don't be scared if you see anything look out of that hole in the bank over there. That's a badger hole. He's about as big as a big 'possum, and his face is striped, black and white...."

46

5

I sat down in the middle of the garden, where snakes could scarcely approach unseen, and leaned my back against a warm yellow pumpkin....

6

All about me giant grasshoppers, twice as big as any I had ever seen, were doing acrobatic feats among the dried vines.

7

The gophers scurried up and down the ploughed ground. There in the sheltered draw bottom the wind did not blow very hard, but I could hear it singing its humming tune up on the level, and I could see the tall grasses wave....

8

I kept as still as I could. Nothing happened. I did not expect anything to happen. I was something that lay under the sun and felt it, like the pumpkins, and I did not want to be anything more. I was entirely happy.

3. ThinkSpeakListen

Describe some of the things that the narrator sees and feels.

The Birdseed Thief

Jason and his mother were true nature lovers. They loved all living things, especially birds. So…they decided to buy a bird feeder for their backyard….

They chose what they thought was a good location….Jason filled the feeder with a variety of food, including sunflower seeds and suet. Before long, the local birds were stopping by….

A week later, however, they saw that….a squirrel had jumped from the big tree to the feeder. It gobbled up the bird food!

Jason and Mom immediately moved the feeder away from the tree. However, that didn't deter the persistent creature….So Jason and Mom placed chicken wire around the feeder to prevent the squirrel from eating the food. Finally, the problem was solved!

4. ThinkSpeakListen

Explain what Jason and his mother did when the squirrel ate the birds' food.

Add Detail with Adjectives

Text	Adjectives	49
A Bird's Free Lunch 	During one <u>terrible</u> night of wind and snow…	
	I fancied him in one of my <u>thick</u> spruces,…his <u>little black</u> feet clinging to the perch,…	
The Shimerdas 	I picked them out of the <u>soft brown</u> earth…	
	I…leaned my back against a <u>warm yellow</u> pumpkin….	
The Birdseed Thief 	Before long, the <u>local</u> birds were stopping by.	
	a squirrel had jumped from the <u>big</u> tree to the feeder.	

5. ThinkSpeakListen

How do adjectives add meaning to sentences?

Being in and Seeing Nature: The Writing of John Burroughs

Slabsides

Writer John Burroughs grew up in Delaware County, New York. He spent most of his life in that area. In summers, he watched the birds and animals from a small cabin in the woods he called "Slabsides." He wrote about the lives of these outdoor creatures, including chipmunks.

The first chipmunk in March is as sure a token of the spring as the first bluebird or the first robin. And it is quite as welcome....

When he emerges in March and is seen upon his little journeys along the fences—or perched upon a log or rock near his hole in the woods—it is another sign that spring is at hand.

The chipmunk is quite a solitary creature. I have never known more than one to occupy the same den. Apparently no two can agree to live together. What a clean, pert, dapper, nervous little fellow he is!...

With his hands spread out upon his breast, he regards you intently! A movement of your arm, and he darts into the wall with a saucy *chip-r-r* sound. It has the effect of slamming the door behind him.

I was much amused one October in watching a chipmunk carry nuts and other food into his den.

He had made a well-defined path from his door out through the weeds and dry leaves....The path was a crooked one.

It dipped under weeds, under some loosely piled stones, under a pile of chestnut posts....

Going and coming, his motions were like clockwork.

He would pause a breath with one foot raised, slip quickly a few yards over some dry leaves, pause again by a stump beside a path, rush across the path to the pile of loose stones...and then dart on to some other cover...where I think he gathered acorns....

In four or five minutes I would see him coming back,...pausing at the same spots, darting over or under the same objects....There was no variation...all the time I observed him.

6. ThinkSpeakListen

Explain why chipmunks gather so many acorns.

One summer day I watched a cat for nearly a half hour trying her arts upon a chipmunk....

Evidently her game was to stalk him...There sat the cat crouched low on the grass, her big, yellow eyes fixed upon the chipmunk,...

and there sat the chipmunk at the mouth of his den, motionless, with his eyes fixed upon the cat. For a long time neither moved....

The chipmunk finally quickly entered his den. The cat soon slunk away.

7. ThinkSpeakListen

Why is the cat watching the chipmunk?

Use Transition Words and Phrases to Connect Events

Transition Words	Event
One summer day	I watched a cat for nearly a half hour trying her arts upon a chipmunk....
For a long time	neither moved....
Sometimes	her head slowly lowered and her eyes seemed to dilate....
The chipmunk finally	quickly entered his den.
The cat soon	slunk away.

8. ThinkSpeakListen

Describe the cat's actions as she stalks the chipmunk.

Waiting for Spring

Each year on February 2, crowds of people eagerly gather in Punxsutawney, Pennsylvania, to watch the famous groundhog known as Punxsutawney Phil. They are there to observe this furry creature emerge from its burrow and predict when spring will arrive....

According to tradition, if it is sunny and Phil sees its shadow, there will be six more weeks of winter weather. If it is cloudy and Phil doesn't see its shadow, spring will come early....

The Groundhog Day tradition began more than a thousand years ago in Europe. Back then, people believed animals that hibernate could predict when spring would come....When these people came to America...they continued the custom....In 1886, February 2 was proclaimed Groundhog Day.

9. ThinkSpeakListen

Explain how Groundhog Day became a tradition in the United States.

Use Commas

When to Use Commas	Example
In series of three or more things (such as adjectives)	What a clean, pert, dapper, nervous little fellow he is!
After transition words and phrases	Going and coming, his motions were like clockwork.
To separate actions or ideas	He would pause a breath with one foot raised, slip quickly a few yards over some dry leaves, pause again by a stump beside a path, rush across the path to the pile of loose stones...and then dart on to some other cover...
When combining sentences	Sometimes her head slowly lowered and her eyes seemed to dilate, and I fancied she was about to spring.

10. ThinkSpeakListen

How do commas help readers understand texts?

Birches a poem by Robert Frost

Robert Frost

In this poem, the poet Robert Frost describes birch trees in winter and summer. The speaker of the poem, the "I", is an adult who thinks back to when he was a boy. He remembers swinging on the birch trees in summer.

When I see birches bend to left
   and right
Across the lines of straighter
   darker trees,
I like to think some boy's been
   swinging them.
But swinging doesn't bend them
   down to stay
As ice-storms do. Often you must
   have seen them
Loaded with ice a sunny winter
   morning
After a rain. They click upon
   themselves
As the breeze rises, and turn
   many-colored....

Soon the sun's warmth makes
   them shed crystal shells
Shattering and avalanching on the
   snow-crust—
Such heaps of broken glass to
   sweep away
You'd think the inner dome of
   heaven had fallen....

One by one he subdued[1] his
    father's trees
By riding them down over and
    over again
Until he took the stiffness out
    of them,
And not one but hung limp, not
    one was left
For him to conquer....

So was I once myself a swinger
    of birches.
And so I dream of going back
    to be....
I'd like to get away from earth
    awhile
And then come back to it and
    begin over....

I'd like to go by climbing a
    birch tree
And climb black branches up a
    snow-white trunk
...till the tree could bear no more,
But dipped its top and set me
    down again.
That would be good both going
    and coming back.

1 subdued—conquered

11. ThinkSpeakListen

Choose a line from the poem and read it aloud. What are some of the
words the poet uses to describe the birch trees?

In Summer by Paul Laurence Dunbar

In this poem, the poet Paul Laurence Dunbar describes the beauty of nature in summer. Like many writers, he uses figures of speech to give his words more meaning.

Paul Laurence Dunbar

Oh, summer has clothed the earth
In a cloak from the loom of the sun!
And a mantle,[1] too, of the skies'
   soft blue,
And a belt where the rivers run.

And now for the kiss of the wind,
And the touch of the air's soft hands,
With the rest from strife and the
   heat of life,
With the freedom of lakes and lands....

1 mantle—something that covers

12. ThinkSpeakListen
What kinds of pictures come to your mind when you read this poem?

Understand Words Using Context Clues

Unfamiliar Word	Clues in Text
swinging	When I see <u>birches bend to left and right</u> Across the lines of <u>straighter</u> darker trees, I like to think some boy's been <u>swinging</u> them.
subdued	One by one he <u>subdued</u> his father's trees By <u>riding them down over and over again</u> Until he <u>took the stiffness out of them</u>, And not one but <u>hung limp</u>, <u>not one was left</u> <u>For him to conquer</u>….
strife	And now for the <u>kiss of the wind</u>, And the touch of the <u>air's soft hands</u>, With the <u>rest from</u> strife and the <u>heat of life</u>,…

13. ThinkSpeakListen

Talk about the photographs that accompany the two poems you read. How did these images help you understand the texts?

Birch Bark Canoes

Birch trees have always grown in the forests of the Northeast. When Native Americans lived in the area long ago, they…valued this gift from nature. They figured out that the outer bark of white birches could be used to make useful things…. However, the most important item they created was the birch bark canoe.

The birch bark canoe was lightweight but sturdy…. Building a birch bark canoe took several weeks. First, the birch bark was peeled from the tree and laid on the ground. Then it was covered with heavy stones to make it flat. Next, it was placed on a frame made of poles and stakes. This formed the shape of the canoe. The ends of the birch bark were then pulled together and tied with root fibers. To make the canoe waterproof, the seams were glued with pine gum and charcoal….

In fact, these traditional canoes were so well designed that they became the models for today's canoes.

14. ThinkSpeakListen
Explain why it took several weeks for the Native Americans to build their birch bark canoes.

Building Research Skills

Prompt

Would you prefer to observe nature in New England or the Mojave Desert? To develop an opinion, conduct research using this guiding question: What are the features of these two regions? Read and take notes from two approved Internet sources.

Question You Will Answer

Research You Will Do

Sources You Will Use

My Research Findings

	New England's Natural Features	Mojave Desert's Natural Features
Source 1	**Facts for Travelers: New England** 1. The region is made up of six U.S. states. 2. The Atlantic Ocean extends along its eastern coast. 3. The region is diverse, with rivers and lakes, forests, mountain ranges, farmlands, beaches.	**National Park Service: Mojave Desert Discovery** 1. The Mojave is a rain shadow desert. It gets very little rain. 2. The desert has many low shrubs. The Joshua Tree is common to this desert. 3. The landscape features low mountains and their basins.
Source 2	**New England Colonies** 1. New England has four seasons. 2. Natural features include rocky coastlines along the Atlantic Ocean. 3. New England includes the Connecticut River Valley and part of the Appalachian Mountains.	**Mojave Desert** 1. The Mojave is a dry desert with very little rain. 2. It has dramatic rock formations and dune fields. 3. The northern section is cold and the southern section is hot.

What do we learn when we look at the world through the eyes of others?

a glass globe

My Language Objectives

- Use exclamation points for effect
- Use progressive verb tenses
- Use precise language to describe
- Write a narrative essay
- Use the language of sequence
- Use sense imagery to describe

My Content Objectives

- Build vocabulary related to character perspective
- Understand what we learn when we look at the world through the eyes of others

Misty and the hen

Lad and the Mistress

63

Here, Boy

An excerpt from *Because of Winn-Dixie* by Kate DiCamillo

At first, I didn't see a dog. There were just a lot of vegetables rolling around on the floor, tomatoes and onions and green peppers....

The manager screamed, "Somebody grab that dog!"

The dog went running over to the manager, wagging his tail and smiling.... Somehow he ended up knocking the manager over. And the manager must have been having a bad day, because lying there on the floor, right in front of everybody, he started to cry....

"Please," said the manager. "Somebody call the pound."

"Wait a minute!" I hollered. "That's my dog. Don't call the pound."

Use Exclamation Points for Effect

At first, I didn't see a dog.

The manager screamed, "Somebody grab that dog!"

"Please," said the manager. "Somebody call the pound."

"Wait a minute!" I hollered.

1. ThinkSpeakListen

What types of emotion might require exclamation points, and what types might not?

Waiting for Stormy

An excerpt from *Stormy, Misty's Foal* by Marguerite Henry

The day at school seemed never-ending. Maureen answered questions like a robot....

In Paul's room, an oral examination was about to take place.... In his mind he was back at Pony Ranch, and Misty had broken out of her stall and gone tearing down the marsh.

And in his fantasy he saw the colt being born; and while it was all wet and new, it was sucked slowly, slowly down into the miry bog....

Tap! Tap! Miss Ogle rapped her pencil sharply on the desk. "Boys and girls," she said, "you have all heard of people suffering from nightmares. But I declare, Paul Beebe is having a *daymare*."...

5

Back home in Misty's shed, all was warm contentment. There was plenty of hay in the manger… and a block of salt hollowed out from many lickings.…

6

She worked at it now in slow delight, her tongue strokes stopping occasionally as she turned to watch a little brown hen rounding out a nest in a corner of the stall.…

7

Out on the marsh Billy Blaze and Watch Eyes, pretending to be stallions, fought and neighed over the little band of mares.

8

Misty looked out at them for a long time, then went to her manger and slowly began munching her hay. The hen, now satisfied with her nest, fluffed out her feathers and settled herself.

2. ThinkSpeakListen

Recount what happens in this story.

A Dog's Life

I sometimes hear it's a dog's life, but even a dog deserves a break, right? Nighttime is falling, and I'm exhausted and ravenous. All I want is a safe haven and something to eat....

I crawl under a park bench and begin to dream of glorious food—hot dogs, ice cream, pizza. Then I awake and my hollow belly is growling....

I head down a dirt road and come to a dark, silent farmhouse.... Sniff, sniff. I can't believe my nose. It's meat and it's first-rate. I can tell by the scent!

I paw open the door to find an entire slab hanging from a pole.... By the time I've eaten three-quarters of it, I'm stuffed fuller than a Thanksgiving turkey, but I keep at it until every single morsel is gone. Satisfied, I settle down for a good night's sleep.

3. ThinkSpeakListen

What feelings does the dog experience in this story? Explain which words from the story point to these feelings.

Use Progressive Verb Tenses

Text	Progressive Verb	Simple Form of Verb
A Dog's Life	Nighttime **is falling**, and I'm exhausted and ravenous.	**falls**

Text	Progressive Verb
A Dog's Life	Then I awake and my hollow belly **is growling**.
Waiting for Stormy	But I declare, Paul Beebe **is having** a *daymare*."
Here, Boy	And the manager **must have been having** a bad day, because lying there on the floor, right in front of everybody, he started to cry.

4. ThinkSpeakListen

Recount the events that occur in "A Dog's Life," using progressive verbs.

Quiet!

An excerpt from *Lad, A Dog:*
A Classic Story of a Courageous Collie

by Albert Payson Terhune

1

It began on a blustery, sour October day. The Mistress had crossed the lake to the village, in her canoe, with Lad curled up in a furry heap in the prow.

On the return trip, about fifty yards from shore, the canoe struck sharply and obliquely against a half-submerged log....

2

Into the ice-chill waters splashed its two occupants.... Swathed and cramped by the folds of her heavy outing skirt, the Mistress was making no progress shoreward.

And the dog flung himself through the water toward her... In a second he had reached her and had caught her sweater-shoulder in his teeth.

70

3

She had the presence of mind to lie out straight, as though she were floating.... The dog's burden was thus made infinitely lighter....

Yet he made scant headway, until she wound one hand in his mane... In this way, by sustained effort that wrenched every giant muscle in the collie's body, they came at last to land.

4

Vastly rejoiced was Lad, and inordinately proud of himself. And the plaudits of the Master and the Mistress were music to him....

Matters soon quieted down; and the incident seemed to end.

Instead, it had just begun.

5. ThinkSpeakListen
Recount what has happened so far in this story.

5 For, within an hour, the Mistress...was stricken with a chill, and by night she was in the first stages of pneumonia....

From the Master's voice and look, Lad understood that something was terribly amiss. Also...he was for the first time in his life forbidden to go into her room...

6 A strange man with a black bag came to the house early in the evening, and he and the Master were closeted for an interminable time in the Mistress's room....

Lad lay down on the threshold, his nose to the crack at the bottom of the door, and waited.

6. ThinkSpeakListen
What different emotions does Lad experience in this story?

Use Precise Language to Describe

meaning:

extremely cold

broader synonym:

cold

Into the **ice-chill** waters splashed its two occupants.

I prefer my lemonade to be ice-chill.

And the dog **flung** himself through the water toward her.

In this way, by sustained effort that **wrenched** every giant muscle in the collie's body, they came at last to land.

A strange man with a black bag came to the house early in the evening, and he and the Master were closeted for an **interminable** time in the Mistress's room.

7. ThinkSpeakListen

Explain why it is important for a writer to use precise language.

Balto, A Heroic Dog

In January 1925, some children in Nome, Alaska, developed a life-threatening disease called diphtheria. There was only one medicine, a serum, that could save them. And it could be found only 1,000 miles away, in Anchorage....

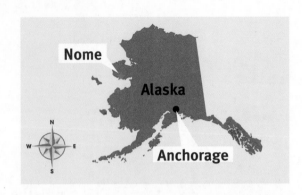

It was decided that the only option was a relay of dogsled teams.... The first musher, or driver, and his team raced with the serum toward Nome. It was the middle of winter, with temperatures as low as 40 degrees below zero....

On February 1, the package was handed off to musher Gunnar Kassen... His team, led by a Siberian husky named Balto, set off to cover the final miles to Nome. A blinding blizzard blew up... However, Balto knew the trail. By following his instincts, he bravely led the team onward. Twenty hours later, they staggered into Nome....The serum had arrived safely.

Gunnar Kassen

8. ThinkSpeakListen

What is the tensest moment in this story? At what moment do you realize that there will be a happy ending?

Write to Sources

Prompt

Imagine that Lad, the dog from "Quiet!", had to guard the farm animals described in "Waiting for Stormy". Using details from both texts, write a first person narrative from Lad's point of view describing what this guard duty would be like.

Topic for Writing

Sources You Will Use

Type of Writing

Purpose for Writing

Sample Essay

I am Lad, the new dog at Paul and Maureen's Chincoteague farm. I spend most of my time at the edge of the fenced-in meadow, watching intently through the fence posts as behind me horses graze and play in the warm sunshine. Once in a while a young colt or filly comes over to greet me, but I always pretend not to hear. I have an important job to do.

> The introduction presents the main character and setting.

The horses used to be offended. They thought I was ignoring them because I felt superior. It's true that this is my farm (well, except when Paul and Maureen are around), but I never thought it was fair that the other animals disliked me for doing my job.

One day, though, one of the farm workers accidentally left the gate latch open. A filly escaped into the field outside. I saw this immediately and darted out after her. I knew that there was a marsh nearby, and if she were to fall into it, she would sink.

> The body paragraphs use description to develop experiences and events. They also show the responses of characters to situations.

Fortunately, I reached her in time, and was able to force her away from the marsh. I guided her back to the farm, to the relief of the other horses.

That day, all the horses realized that I don't ignore them because I think I'm better than them. I just have an important job to do, and I have to avoid any distractions. That way, if there is an emergency, I can notice it immediately and spring into action.

> The conclusion provides resolution and wraps up the narrative.

75

My Breaking In
An excerpt from *Black Beauty*

by Anna Sewell

Every one may not know what breaking in is, therefore I will describe it. It means to teach a horse to wear a saddle and bridle. And to carry on his back a man, woman or child…

Besides this he has to learn to wear a collar, a crupper, and a breeching, and to stand still while they are put on.…

My master gave me some oats as usual, and after a good deal of coaxing he got the bit into my mouth. Then he got the bridle fixed, but it was a nasty thing!…

At least I thought so; but I knew my mother always wore one when she went out. And all horses did when they were grown up, so…I got to wear my bit and bridle.

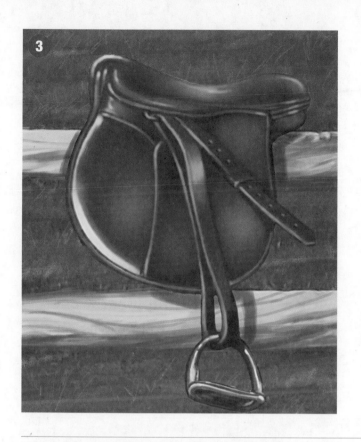

Next came the saddle, but that was not half so bad. My master put it on my back very gently...

One morning, my master got on my back and rode me round the meadow...It certainly did feel odd, but I must say I felt rather proud to carry my master....

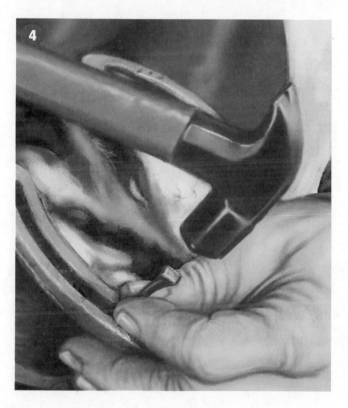

The next unpleasant business was putting on the iron shoes.... The blacksmith took my feet in his hand, one after the other...

Then he took a piece of iron the shape of my foot, and clapped it on. Next, he drove some nails through the shoe quite into my hoof so that the shoe was firmly on....

9. ThinkSpeakListen

What different feelings has Black Beauty expressed so far in this passage?

And now having got so far, my master went on to break me to harness. There were more new things to wear. First, a stiff heavy collar just on my neck, and a bridle…

Next, there was a small saddle with a nasty stiff strap that went right under my tail. That was the crupper.

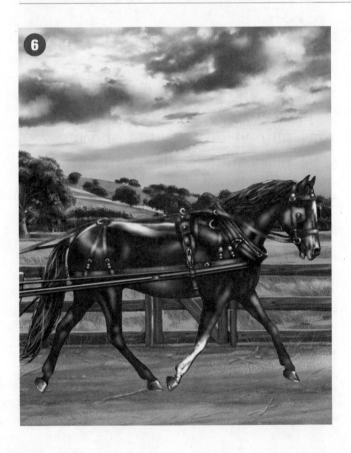

I hated the crupper. To have my long tail doubled up and poked through that strap was almost as bad as the bit. I never felt more like kicking, but of course I could not kick such a good master.

And so in time I got used to everything, and could do my work as well as my mother.

10. ThinkSpeakListen

Why do you think Black Beauty keeps mentioning his mother?

78

Use the Language of Sequence

The **next** unpleasant business was putting on the iron shoes.

Then he took a piece of iron the shape of my foot, and clapped it on.

Next, he drove some nails through the shoe quite into my hoof so that the shoe was firmly on.

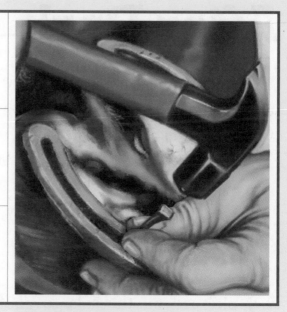

And **now** having got so far, my master went on to break me to harness.

First, a stiff heavy collar just on my neck, and a bridle.

Next, there was a small saddle with a nasty stiff strap that went right under my tail.

11. ThinkSpeakListen

Recount the events of your day so far. Use the language of sequence.

After Dark

When Uncle Marcos came to visit last month, he gave me a little book... The title was *After Dark: Nocturnal Animals*. "What's a nocturnal animal?" I asked. "It's simple," said Uncle Marcos. "It's an animal that rests during the day and becomes active at night."...

I plopped on the sofa to gobble up the book like a juicy, red apple. Mr. Ruggles, my dog, curled up beside me, and Uncle Marcos tossed a pair of night vision goggles at me. "Let's do some fieldwork first. It's getting dark outside!"

We tiptoed to the woods on the edge of our backyard... We slipped on the goggles. With them, the animals would be visible in the dark.

Suddenly, a single mouse scrambled from behind a rock. Not a second later, an owl with oversized eyes swooped down quickly and snatched it up in its claws.... I couldn't stand to watch! Fortunately, Mr. Ruggles started barking and yelping, which startled the owl into dropping his helpless prey.

12. ThinkSpeakListen

What other types of animals might you see in the woods with night vision goggles?

Use Sense Imagery to Describe

Sentence	Imagery	Type of Imagery
First, a **stiff heavy collar** just on my neck, and a bridle.	**stiff heavy collar**	tactile

I plopped on the sofa to gobble up the book like a juicy, **red** apple.

Fortunately, Mr. Ruggles started **barking** and **yelping**...

How do we make decisions about developing new technology?

solar panels

My Language Objectives

- Use quotation marks in dialogue
- Connect ideas with coordinating conjunctions
- Condense ideas with relative pronouns
- Use compound adjectives
- Form nouns from verbs
- Write an opinion essay

Content Objectives

- Build vocabulary related to energy sources and solutions
- Understand the debate about energy sources and their effect on the environment

public transportation

charging station for electric cars

83

Town Tackles Energy Debate by Francisco Blane

The following excerpts come from a fictional newspaper called the Hopeville Ledger. Hopeville's mayor, Julia Sanchez, held a town meeting to discuss plans for a new power plant.

"The federal government will give us $200 million," Sanchez said. "But that will only pay part of the cost.... The question is what kind of energy plant will we develop?"...

Tom Bradshaw, a professor..., said, "We must pursue solar power. Solar power is energy from the sun. It's free and clean. We can't continue to release greenhouse gases..."

However, real estate developer Carlos Hill cautioned against solar power. "The Mesa Palms solar plant two counties over cost $2 billion. We can build a natural gas plant for half that amount."...

"We all have our statistics, Mr. Hill," said Eve Pearce, a spokesperson for Lightpath Energy. "The Mesa Palms solar plant was expensive. But it generates enough power for 100,000 homes—more than you need!"

1. ThinkSpeakListen

Explain the energy choices the Hopeville citizens are discussing.

Use Quotation Marks in Dialogue

Who spoke?	What did that person say?
1 Julia Sanchez, Mayor	"The federal government will give us $200 million," Sanchez said. "But that will only pay part of the cost."
2 Tom Bradshaw, Professor	Tom Bradshaw, a professor…, said, "We must pursue solar power…. We can't continue to release greenhouse gases that cause the planet to overheat."
3 Carlos Hill, Real Estate Developer	However, real estate developer Carlos Hill cautioned against solar power. "The Mesa Palms solar plant two counties over cost $2 billion. We can build a natural gas plant for half that amount."
4 Eve Pearce, Spokesperson	"We all have our statistics, Mr. Hill," said Eve Pearce, a spokesperson for Lightpath Energy. "The Mesa Palms solar plant was expensive. But it generates enough power for 100,000 homes…"

2. ThinkSpeakListen

Summarize the different opinions expressed by Hopeville's citizens. Which opinion do you agree with most?

The Hopeville Ledger
Editorial Pages

The editorial pages of a newspaper print letters written by readers. Often, readers will want to respond to an article they've read in the newspaper.

Sunshine Is Free: Go Solar!

Hopeville should build a solar plant. Sunshine is free. And unlike nonrenewable fossil fuels, sunshine will always be available....

A solar plant is costly. But it will power clean energy to tens of thousands of homes, or more....

It may be true, as Mr. Hill said, that we still have plenty of fossil fuels. But fossil fuels won't last forever.

Nonrenewable means they cannot be replaced. Someday, they will be gone. We need to be ready when that happens.

Natural Gas: The Natural Choice for Hopeville

I am not against solar power, but Hopeville needs a more cost-effective power source. Natural gas is the better choice right now. It's available and much more affordable....

Plus, natural gas produces just half the carbon dioxide of our current coal-burning power plant.... That means even less carbon dioxide in the atmosphere.

Too Many Statistics, Too Few Facts

Some people said solar power is too expensive. Their only evidence was the Mesa Palms solar plant. That plant was built five years ago, and it is just one example. Have they looked at others?...

Some people said natural gas causes too much pollution. But is that true? I've heard conflicting evidence....

We should study the facts carefully. Then we can decide.

3. ThinkSpeakListen
Which of these opinion letters do you agree with? Explain why.

Fossil Fuels: What's the Story?

Millions of years ago, Earth was covered by water. When plants and animals died, they sank to the ocean floor.... Eventually, the fossils of the plants and animals turned into oil, coal, and natural gas. Today, we burn these products for fuel. That's why oil, coal, and natural gas are called "fossil fuels."

plant fossil

So what's the problem?... When we burn a fossil fuel to generate electricity or power a car, boat, or plane, we release the carbon stored in the fuel.... Carbon dioxide, or CO_2, is a greenhouse gas.... An increase in CO_2 in the atmosphere can cause Earth's temperature to rise, changing our planet's climate.

What's being done? Many nations... are looking to wind and solar power, for example, to help meet the world's energy needs.

4. ThinkSpeakListen
Explain what happens when fossil fuels are burned.

Connect Ideas with Coordinating Conjunctions

Yes, fossil fuels are nonrenewable, **but** they are still available.

It may be true…that we still have plenty of fossil fuels. **But** fossil fuels won't last forever.

That plant was built five years ago, **and** it is just one example.

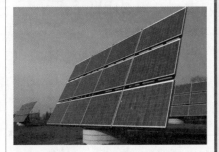

Sunshine is free. **And** unlike nonrenewable fossil fuels, sunshine will always be available.

Today, we burn these products for fuel.…
So what's the problem?

5. ThinkSpeakListen

What are two advantages of sunshine as a source of energy?

Green Transportation Solutions

by Brooke Harris

A typical car travels an average of 19,000 kilometers (12,000 miles) per year.... Covering that kind of territory takes a lot of energy. Most of it comes from burning oil and gas. These fuels, called fossil fuels, are in a limited, and dwindling, supply.

Burning fossil fuels also produces air pollution, such as when a truck belches a cloud of black smoke. Even worse, burning fossil fuels releases carbon dioxide, a gas.

Carbon dioxide and other gases float high into the sky. They trap the sun's heat, like a greenhouse, and raise the planet's temperature. This is called global warming. The result is climate change, which has been linked to extremes in weather...

Fortunately,... "green" technologies are being developed. Some of these technologies reduce or replace fossil fuels burned by cars. Other technologies lower people's dependence on cars.

In a June 2013 speech, President Barack Obama said, "I'm announcing a new national climate action plan… to keep the United States of America a global leader in the fight against climate change."…

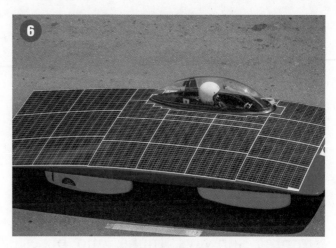

He…encouraged further development of battery-powered and hybrid cars that run on gas or batteries. Both types of these "green" cars are already on the roads.

BIODIESEL FUEL
$4.99

Running cars with "green" fuels such as biodiesel or ethanol may be a better choice than using fossil fuels. Biodiesel fuel is made from soybeans, palm oil, and other plants. Ethanol is made from corn and sugar.

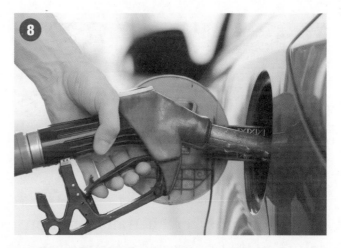

Unlike fossil fuels, green fuels use renewable sources. They also emit fewer greenhouse gases. According to the Renewable Fuels Association, "using ethanol in place of gasoline helps to reduce carbon dioxide emissions by up to 30–50%."…

6. ThinkSpeakListen

Summarize how "green" fuels are different from fossil fuels.

9

Running subways, trains, and buses takes energy. Often, that energy comes from burning fossil fuels. But the cost to the environment per person is considerably less....

10

The Washington, D.C., Orange Line...is a model of transportation planning.... Tens of thousands of people today ride the Orange Line to their jobs...

11

There's another green transportation solution that's simple, effective, and right in front of your eyes—your own two feet! Walking and bicycling eliminate the need for cars and public transportation....

12

Heatherwood Elementary School... more than tripled the number of kids who now walk and bike to school.... Walking and biking... send children on their way to the sixty minutes of daily exercise recommended by the American Public Health Association.

7. ThinkSpeakListen

Talk about how you travel to school. Is it a "green" solution?

Condense Ideas with Relative Pronouns

Instead of two sentences...	use one sentence with a relative pronoun
1. The result is climate change. 2. This change has been linked to extremes in weather.	1. The result is climate change, <u>which</u> has been linked to extremes in weather.
1. He...encouraged further development of battery-powered and hybrid cars. 2. These cars run on gas or batteries.	1. He...encouraged further development of battery-powered and hybrid cars <u>that</u> run on gas or batteries.
1. There's another green transportation solution. 2. It's simple, effective, and right in front of your eyes—your own two feet!	1. There's another green transportation solution <u>that's</u> simple, effective, and right in front of your eyes—your own two feet!

8. ThinkSpeakListen

Explain some of the effects of climate change.

The Solar Challenge

My team's solar-powered car reached the finals in the World Solar Challenge and we headed to Australia for the race. Teams from all over the world were there. Luckily for us, there were only four other high school teams. Most of the other competitors were universities or corporations....

The race was all about solar energy!...

To win, we would have to drive about 700 kilometers a day, close to 450 miles!

The first day we were doing well. The college teams were beating us, but we were leading all the high school teams! We were worried when clouds covered the sun for hours, almost draining our solar battery. Fortunately, the sun came out again...

Victory! We didn't win the overall race, but we had the best time of the high school teams. The crowd roared its congratulations. We'll definitely be back next year!

9. ThinkSpeakListen

Explain why the team was worried when the clouds covered the sun.

Use Compound Adjectives

	Adjective	Adjective + Noun
	plug-in	plug-in cars
	long-term	long-term solution
	battery-powered	battery-powered cars
	low-tech	low-tech solution

10. ThinkSpeakListen

Summarize the advantages and disadvantages of a battery-powered car.

Opinions About Green Transportation

In "Green Transportation Solutions," Brooke Harris presents several solutions to pollution from automobiles. Which solution is the "best"? Four writers express their opinions and give their reasons.

Opinion 1: Solar Power for a Bright Future

The best green transportation solution is the use of solar cars that people can afford. Solar-powered vehicles use no fossil fuels....

Although battery-powered cars do not burn fossil fuels, "Power plants that make electricity to charge the car's battery" do.

Hybrid cars reduce people's use of fossil fuel, but they don't eliminate it. And cars that run on renewable fuels...still emit carbon dioxide (CO_2). Solar-powered vehicles emit no carbon dioxide....

Subways and buses...mean fewer cars on city streets, but they don't meet the needs of everyone. Not only that, but buses and trains still rely on some fossil fuel.

11. ThinkSpeakListen
Summarize Opinion 1.

Opinion 2: Catch a Seat on the Bus

Solar cars are still experimental. Hybrid and biodiesel cars are very expensive, so most people cannot afford them. On the other hand, public transportation is affordable. It meets the needs of many people....

Public transportation takes cars off the roads. Harris cites New York City's Green Dividend report. It states, "Residents save $19 billion per year because they own fewer cars and drive less than average Americans."

Opinion 3: Fight Pollution and Get Fit

The solution that makes the most sense is the low-tech one. People who can walk or ride a bike should stop using forms of transportation that burn fossil fuels. If everyone who could do this made that choice, the planet would benefit and so would they....

Heatherwood Elementary School more than tripled the number of students who walked and biked to school—from 12 to 43 percent....

By walking or biking, people help the planet and improve their health.

Opinion 4: No Single Solution Can Solve a Big Problem

There is no "best" solution to reduce carbon dioxide emissions…. While many people in cities could choose public transportation, some people cannot. For those who can't, green cars are the answer….

Many Americans can use public transportation. In New York City, five million people ride the subway every day. Because they are on the subway, they are not in a car….

People who commute short distances …do not need subways and buses to stay out of cars. As Harris states, "Walking and bicycling eliminate the need for cars and public transportation."…

Green cars, public transportation, and "biped power" are each a partial solution to a big problem. Together, however, these three solutions can make a big impact on people and our planet.

12. ThinkSpeakListen

Do you think there is one "green" transportation solution to reduce carbon emissions? Or is there more than one solution?

Form Nouns from Verbs

Verb	Noun
walk, bike	By <u>walking</u> or <u>biking</u>, people help the planet and improve their health.
walk, bicycle	As Harris states, "<u>Walking</u> and <u>bicycling</u> eliminate the need for cars and public transportation."

13. ThinkSpeakListen

Would you prefer to walk or bike to school? Explain why.

America's Greenest City

In my opinion, the city of Portland, Oregon, is one of the greenest cities in America....

Each day, about a quarter of Portland workers commute by bike, car pool, or public transportation. Of these, 10,000 people bike to work on the city's 1,106 kilometers (700 miles) of bicycle paths....

Portlanders now recycle two-thirds of their waste. That's one of the highest rates in the United States....

Portland was also the first U.S. city to adopt a Global Warming Action Plan. Following this plan, Portland and the surrounding area were able to curb greenhouse gases by almost 13 percent....

If all this hasn't convinced you that Portland is the nation's greenest city, consider this. The city has 10,000 acres of parkland.... These parks help make Portland a truly green city!

14. ThinkSpeakListen

Explain why the writer describes Portland as one of the greenest cities in America.

Writing to Sources

In "Opinions About Green Transportation" and the *Hopeville Ledger* Editorial Pages, you read other people's opinions on green energy. Choose an editorial you disagree with, and write a response in which you argue against the opinion expressed by the writer. Make sure to support your opinion with concrete facts, details, and examples from at least two texts in this unit.

Sources You Will Use

Type of Writing: Opinion

Type of Evidence You Will Use

Sample Essay

I disagree with the author of Opinion 2, who says that "public transportation is the 'green' solution that makes the most sense today." There are several solutions available today to reduce carbon emissions, and we must try them all.

> **Writer introduces topic and states opinion.**

It may be true that green cars are not "perfect solutions," as the writer of Opinion 1 says. But these cars release less carbon dioxide into the air than the cars on the road that run on fossil fuels. For example, hybrid cars have lower carbon dioxide emissions than typical cars on the road. Cars that run on renewable fuels also emit less carbon dioxide. The writer of Opinion 4 says, "A car that runs on ethanol emits from 30 to 50 percent less carbon dioxide than a fossil-fuel burning car."

> **Writer supports opinion with reasons and evidence.**

Another way to reduce emissions from fossil fuels is to walk and bicycle when possible instead of getting in a car. Writer Brooke Harris calls this a "low-tech" solution that everyone can do. She says, "There's another green transportation solution that's simple, effective, and right in front of your eyes—your own two feet!"

> **Writer supports opinion with reasons and evidence.**

Finally, public transportation is also an important green solution. It is affordable and "meets the needs of many people," says the writer of Opinion 2. And when people use buses and trains, they keep cars off the road.

In summary, to solve a big problem like carbon emissions, we need more than one solution. We have to try everything—from cars to bikes to buses.

> **Writer restates opinion and makes a concluding statement.**

How do we overcome obstacles?

My Language Objectives

- Use the language of sequence
- Use prepositional phrases
- Use commonly confused words
- Building research skills
- Use noun phrases to enrich meaning
- Produce complete sentences

My Content Objectives

- Build vocabulary related to overcoming challenges
- Understand ways in which people can surmount obstacles

the valiant little tailor

102

Rabbit

Molly Whuppie and the king

103

Rabbit and Coyote

This tale tells the story of Rabbit and Coyote. Rabbit came upon a big rock and once there, he decided to deceive, or trick, Coyote... Soon Coyote came by and Rabbit leaned against the big rock.

"What are you doing, brother?" Coyote asked Rabbit....

"Come here quickly, brother, for the sky is falling down on us. You must lean against the rock and then hold it up while I go search for a stick that will prop up the sky."

Coyote, of course, agreed and began holding up the rock with all his might... Rabbit simply left Coyote holding the rock...

Coyote shouted, "Come back, brother! The weight of the rock is making me tired." But Rabbit did not come back. He ignored Coyote's pleas.

1. ThinkSpeakListen

Why might Rabbit want to trick Coyote?

Use the Language of Sequence

Event	Word or Phrase That Indicates Sequence	Event
Rabbit came upon a big rock and	**once there,**	he decided to deceive, or trick, Coyote.
Rabbit came upon a big rock and once there, he decided to deceive, or trick, Coyote.	**Soon**	Coyote came by and Rabbit leaned against the big rock.
You must lean against the rock and then hold it up	**while**	I go search for a stick that will prop up the sky."
Rabbit simply left Coyote holding the rock	**When**	Rabbit didn't return, Coyote shouted, "Come back, brother!"

2. ThinkSpeakListen

Describe the events of your day so far. Use at least three of the sequence indicators listed above.

The Valiant Little Tailor

by the Brothers Grimm

A tailor spread jam on his bread. He laid the bread near him, and continued happily sewing.

In the meantime, the smell of the sweet jam attracted flies in great numbers....

He got a bit of cloth from the hole under his worktable, and struck the flies. When he drew the cloth away and counted, there lay before him seven dead, with legs stretched out. He could not help admiring his own bravery.

And so the little tailor hastened to cut himself a belt and stitched it. Finally, he embroidered on it in large letters, "Seven At One Stroke."

The brave little tailor wanted to tell the world... His heart wagged with joy like a lamb's tail....

He took to the road boldly. And as he was light and nimble, he felt no fatigue.

The road led him up a mountain, and when he had reached the highest point, he met up with a powerful giant looking about him quite comfortably.

The little tailor went bravely up and spoke to the giant. He said, "Good day, comrade, you are sitting there overlooking the world!"

3. ThinkSpeakListen
What can we tell about the tailor's personality from this part of the story?

Chi Li and the Serpent

Many moons ago, a ferocious serpent lived in a mountain above a Chinese village. One day, to the villagers' dismay, the giant snake came down from its cave and demanded half their rice. The terrified people quickly complied....

This went on every year for nine years until a girl named Chi Li said, "Enough! I will put an end to this!"...

She set out with a hound, a sword, and a bag of sweetened rice balls. As she neared the serpent's lair, she laid the rice balls sideways along the path. Then she and the hound hid. Drawn by the scent, the serpent soon slithered forth. It devoured one rice ball, and then another. The hound dashed out and ran wildly around the snake in a circle...until the serpent was so dizzy that it toppled over.

Chi Li...chopped off the serpent's head. The villagers hailed her as a hero, and everyone lived peacefully from then on.

4. ThinkSpeakListen

What are the problem and solution in this story?

Use Prepositional Phrases

Sentence	Prepositional Phrase	Question the Prepositional Phrase Answers
In the meantime, the smell of the sweet jam attracted flies **in great numbers**.	In the meantime	**When** are the flies attracted?
	in great numbers	**How many** flies are there?
When he drew the cloth away and counted, there lay **before him** seven dead, with legs stretched out.	before him	**Where** are the flies lying?
His heart wagged **with joy** like a lamb's tail.	with joy	**Why** does the tailor's heart wag?
The little tailor went bravely up and spoke **to the giant**.	to the giant	**To whom** does the tailor speak?

5. ThinkSpeakListen

Describe the tailor in three sentences, using at least one prepositional phrase in each sentence. Then, determine what question each prepositional phrase answers.

Molly Whuppie

an adaptation of a Scottish fairy tale

Once upon a time there was a couple who had too many children and they could not feed them, so they took the three youngest and left them in the woods.

The girls wandered through the dark, frightening woods until they came upon a house.... The woman inside said, "I can't let you in. My husband is a giant with a terrible temper. You can't be here when he comes home."

The girls begged harder... So the woman finally let them in and fed them, but just as they had begun to eat, a dreadful voice said: "Fee, fie, fo, fum, I smell the blood of some earthly ones."

And suddenly, before the girls could escape, the giant entered the house.

3

The giant demanded to know who was in their home, and the wife said, "It's three poor, cold, and hungry girls who will go once they eat...."

The giant grunted, ate up a big supper, and then ordered the girls to stay. Now the giant had three daughters of his own, and the lost girls were to sleep in the same room with the giant's daughters.

4

The youngest of the three lost girls was called Molly Whuppie.... She noticed that before they went to bed, the giant put straw ropes around her neck and her sisters' necks, but he put gold chains around his own daughters' necks.

Molly knew not to fall asleep. When she was sure all the others, especially the giant, were asleep, Molly slipped out of bed.

6. ThinkSpeakListen
What feelings has the giant's wife experienced so far in the story?

She then quickly exchanged the straw ropes on her and her sisters' necks for the gold chains that were on the giant's daughters' necks.

No one woke up during the exchange and so Molly let out a deep sigh and fell asleep.

In the night, the giant got up. He felt for the necks with straw and picked up his daughters. As they cried out, Molly and her sisters escaped.

The girls ran and ran, and never stopped on their quest for safety until they saw a grand house before them. It turned out to be a king's house.

7. ThinkSpeakListen

Describe what has happened so far in this story.

Use Commonly Confused Words

Commonly Confused Words		Correct Use in a Sentence	Word Meaning
	their	The giant demanded to know who was in **their** home, and the wife said, "It's three poor, cold, and hungry girls who will go once they eat…"	"belonging to them"
	there	"Good day, comrade, you are sitting **there** overlooking the world!"	"in that place"
	it's	"**It's** three poor, cold, and hungry girls who will go once they eat…."	"it is"
	its	One day, to the villagers' dismay, the giant snake came down from **its** cave and demanded half their rice.	"belonging to it"

8. ThinkSpeakListen

Explain the difference between "their" and "there," and the difference between "it's" and "its." Create example sentences using each one correctly.

Kate Shelley: A Young Hero

A fierce storm was raging on a summer evening in 1881 in Moingona, Iowa. The waters were rising in Honey Creek. Kate Shelley...heard a locomotive approaching. Suddenly, there was a loud crash as the locomotive plunged off the washed-out bridge into the creek below....

...She was relieved to see that two members of the crew had escaped... However, Kate realized that the midnight express train from Ogden was due soon. She had to do something, or it, too, was doomed.

She...would have to get to the Moingona station and tell them to hold the train from Ogden. To reach Moingona, Kate had to cross a long, high train bridge over the turbulent Des Moines River.... At last she made it. Kate raced the remaining half-mile to Moingona, and told the agent about the bridge....

The station was able to hold the train from Ogden.

9. ThinkSpeakListen
What character traits did Kate Shelley display during the rainstorm?

Building Research Skills

Prompt

Research subject

Research question

Research goal

Final product

Imagine that you have been asked to write a story from the point of view of a legendary giant from folk literature. One of your guiding research questions is: Who are the most famous giants and what are they like? Read and take notes from two or more sources to help you answer this question. List the sources of your information.

Paraphrasing to Avoid Plagiarism

Original Text	Synonyms and Restatements
"Run away," said she. "My husband the giant will eat you up, bones and all. The last boy who came here stole two bags of gold. So off with you!"	The giant's wife seems concerned for Jack's safety and is warning him how dangerous her husband is.
Yet the giantess **kindly** allowed Jack to come into the kitchen, and set before him a giant breakfast.	Even though this danger exists, the giant's wife also cares enough for Jack that she wants to feed him breakfast.
	kindly – warmly, compassionately, generously

Paraphrase

The giant's wife is concerned for Jack's safety. She warns him away from her home, since her husband is dangerous. However, she is also generous and compassionate, and agrees to give Jack breakfast.

Hercules' Quest
an excerpt from "The Three Golden Apples"

by Nathaniel Hawthorne

Hercules, in order to complete his quest, had to get three golden apples. He asked the giant, Atlas, about the apples and how he might get them....

"If it were not for this little business of holding up the sky, I would make half a dozen steps across the sea, and get them for you," said Atlas.

"You are very kind," replied Hercules. "Can't you rest the sky upon a mountain?"

"None of them are quite high enough," said Atlas, shaking his head.... "What if you should take my burden on your shoulders, while I do your errand for you?"

Now Hercules was a remarkably strong man....

"Well, then," answered Hercules, "I will climb the mountain behind you there, and relieve you of your burden."

So without more words, the sky was shifted from the shoulders of Atlas, and placed upon those of Hercules.

When this was safely accomplished, the first thing that the giant did was to stretch himself.... Then, all at once, he began to caper, and leap, and dance, for joy at his freedom. When his joy had a little subsided, he stepped into the sea.

Hercules watched the giant, as he still went onward until at last the gigantic shape faded entirely out of view.

10. ThinkSpeakListen

Why does Atlas offer to help Hercules?

And now Hercules began to consider what he should do, in case Atlas should be drowned in the sea.... If any such misfortune were to happen, how could he...get rid of the sky?...

Finally, Hercules beheld the huge shape of the giant... At his nearer approach, Atlas held up his hand, in which Hercules could perceive three magnificent golden apples, as big as pumpkins, all hanging from one branch.

"I am glad to see you again," shouted Hercules, when the giant was within hearing. "So you have got the golden apples?"

"Certainly, certainly," answered Atlas; "and very fair apples they are. I took the finest that grew on the tree..."

11. ThinkSpeakListen

What is Hercules feeling at this point in the story? Cite text evidence to back up your ideas.

Use Noun Phrases to Enrich Meaning

| "If it were not for this little business of holding up the sky, I would make **half a dozen steps** across the sea, and get them for you," said Atlas. | Hercules watched the giant, as he still went onward until at last **the gigantic shape** faded entirely out of view. | Finally, Hercules beheld **the huge shape** of the giant… |

Point of Emphasis:
Atlas's large size

At his nearer approach, Atlas held up his hand, in which Hercules could perceive **three magnificent golden apples**, as big as pumpkins, all hanging from one branch….

"Certainly, certainly," answered Atlas; "and **very fair apples** they are. I took the finest that grew on the tree…"

12. ThinkSpeakListen

Describe the room that you are in. Remember to enrich your sentences by adding adjectives to nouns and noun phrases.

Paul Bunyan and the Troublesome Mosquitoes

Paul Bunyan was a giant of a human being. As a baby, he was so enormous that he had to sleep in a lumber wagon instead of a crib....

Paul grew up to become a famous lumberjack. He was so powerful that he could fell twelve trees in a single stroke....

Remember the summer of the troublesome mosquitoes? Well, those mosquitoes were mean, and they had a painful bite!...

However, Paul was a resourceful man. He imported some huge bees to destroy the pesky mosquitoes. Unfortunately, that just made things worse. The fearsome insects intermarried and had children that could sting like a bee and bite as often as a mosquito!

Their craving for sweets was their downfall.... A ship came up the river, bringing sugar to the lumber camp. The greedy insects swarmed the decks and ate so much sugar that they couldn't fly. They plummeted into the river and drowned.

13. ThinkSpeakListen
Did Paul Bunyan's large size help him to get rid of the mosquitoes? Explain why or why not.

Produce Complete Sentences

Complete Sentence	
Paul grew up to become a famous lumberjack.	
Subject	**Verb**
Paul	grew up

Paul Bunyan was a giant of a human being.	Unfortunately, that just made things worse.
He imported some huge bees to destroy the pesky mosquitoes.	They plummeted into the river and drowned.

14. ThinkSpeakListen

Summarize the rules for determining whether a sentence is complete, and discuss why you think it is important to write in complete sentences.

Essential Question
How do communities evolve?

a Native American camp

My Language Objectives

- Use subordinate clauses in sentences
- Connect a sequence of events
- Use pronouns to refer to nouns
- Write an informative essay
- Use adjectives to add detail to nouns
- Expand sentences with adverbs

My Content Objectives

- Build vocabulary related to the development of communities in the United States
- Understand early developments in U.S. transportation and migration

a wagon train

Route 66

123

The Open Road

by Monica Halpern

The first automobiles appeared in the 1890s.... At that time, there were only 144 miles of paved roads in the nation. When people went for a drive, most bounced along dirt tracks....

Then in 1908, Henry Ford introduced the Model T automobile.... Because it didn't cost much, many people bought it. As more people owned cars, the need for paved roads, gas stations, and new maps increased....

People with cars...wanted to hit the open road and explore America.... So in 1916 Congress passed the Federal-Aid Road Act. It made funds available to help states build two-lane interstate highways....

Route 66 was one of the first good roads. In the 1920s it linked small towns and big cities from Chicago to Los Angeles.

1. ThinkSpeakListen

Summarize the key facts about the first cars and roads in the United States.

Use Subordinate Clauses in Sentences

Subordinate Clause	Main Clause
When people went for a drive,	most bounced along dirt tracks.
Because it didn't cost much,	many people bought it.
As more people owned cars,	the need for paved roads, gas stations, and new maps increased.

2. ThinkSpeakListen

Explain what happened after the Model T was introduced.

Dust Bowl Refugees

Beginning in 1931, the Great Plains region began suffering from drought. After months without rain, soil that used to be fertile became arid and barren.... Then heavy winds caused a series of dust storms to ravage the Midwest.

In 1933 alone there were around thirty-eight documented dust storms, or black blizzards. By 1934, the area seemed like a desert. Then on April 14, 1935, Black Sunday happened. Winds began to blow and the worst black blizzard hit.

Finally, when the blizzard stopped, more than 400,000 people had lost their homes and farms. These "dust bowl refugees"...had no choice but to flee the Great Plains and relocate.

Many hit the road and migrated to the Northwest, emigrating to California, Washington, or Oregon. They hoped the open roads would lead to a better life.

"Dust Bowl Refugee" music and lyrics by Woody Guthrie

From the south land and the
  drought land,
Come the wife and kids and me,
And this old world is a hard world
For a dust bowl refugee.

Yes, we ramble and we roam
And the highway that's our home,
It's a never-ending highway
For a dust bowl refugee.

Yes, we wander and we work
In your crops and in your fruit,
Like the whirlwinds on the desert
That's the dust bowl refugees.

I'm a dust bowl refugee,
I'm a dust bowl refugee,
And I wonder will I always
Be a dust bowl refugee?

3. ThinkSpeakListen

Describe what life was like for "dust bowl refugees" in Woody Guthrie's song.

Black Sunday: An Eyewitness Account

April 14, 1935, is the date of the worst dust storm in our nation's history, now known as Black Sunday. Pauline Winkler Grey, who lived with her husband in Meade County, Kansas, gives this first person account of what happened that day.

"I rushed to the window.... On the south there was blue sky, golden sunlight and tranquility; on the north, there was a menacing curtain of boiling black dust....

We stood in our living room in pitch blackness.... Finally, we groped our way to the wall switch and turned on the light...."

"When we flipped the switch again, we could see only a dark brown mass of soil pressed tightly against the outside of the glass.... The wind gradually subsided... but fine particles of wheat-land soil sifted down from the sky."

4. ThinkSpeakListen
Describe Pauline Winkler Grey's experience on April 14, 1935. How is a firsthand account different from a third person account of the same experience?

Connect a Sequence of Events

1. **Beginning in 1931**, the Great Plains region began suffering from drought.

2. **Then** heavy winds caused a series of dust storms to ravage the Midwest.

3. **In 1933** alone there were around thirty-eight documented dust storms, or black blizzards.

4. **By 1934,** the area seemed like a desert.

5. **Then on April 14, 1935,** Black Sunday happened…and the worst black blizzard hit.

6. **Finally,** when the blizzard stopped, more than 400,000 people had lost their homes and farms.

5. ThinkSpeakListen

Talk about how the Dust Bowl began. Then recount the time line of events leading to the end of the blizzard.

Building the Transcontinental Railroad

by Andrea Matthews

In 1830 the first railroad in the United States opened in Baltimore, and it had just 21 kilometers (13 miles) of track. Other railroad lines were built, mostly in the Northeast. Soon the East Coast was crisscrossed with train tracks, connecting cities.

By the 1850s, railroads were changing cities. For example, in 1850 Chicago had 30,000 people and one railroad. By 1856 the city had ten railroads, and by 1860 its population had tripled due to the rail system.

A few dreamers wanted to expand the railroad to the lightly settled West, but there was little demand for it. Then gold was discovered in California in 1848. Word spread and people rushed there to look for gold.

Travelers crossed the plains in covered wagons or sailed around South America to reach California. Either way, the trip took four months or more. People wanted a better way to travel to the West.

Theodore Judah

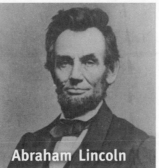
Abraham Lincoln

Theodore Judah was a young engineer who...believed that a transcontinental railroad could and should be built....

Judah...convinced President Abraham Lincoln to sign the Pacific Railroad Act of 1862....

The Central Pacific Railroad Company would begin in California, laying track east. The Union Pacific Railroad Company would start at the Missouri River, laying track west. They would meet somewhere in the middle.... Either way, the race was on.

Who were these amazing workers?... There were Irish, German, Chinese, and Swedish workers. Others were former enslaved laborers or ex-soldiers.... They built tunnels through mountains, laid rail across deserts, and dug through snowstorms, mudslides, and avalanches.

People had expected the transcontinental railroad to be completed in 1876. Instead, it was completed in 1869, seven years early. The two railroad companies that had laid the tracks agreed to meet to lay the last rail at Promontory Point, Utah, on May 10.

6. ThinkSpeakListen

Explain how the railroad was built by the two railroad companies.

On the big day, hundreds of people gathered. The governor of California, Leland Stanford, drove in the golden spike that joined together the Central Pacific and Union Pacific railroads.

The transcontinental railroad changed the nation. By linking East with West, the railroad helped unite the nation. Americans began to feel they were citizens of the United States, not just members of their local community.

The progress of the railroad was not celebrated by all. The Plains Indians were opposed to workers laying track across their sacred land…. The land, and the American bison, or buffalo, that roamed the land were essential to their way of life….

However, the bison damaged tracks and got in the way of the trains, so railroad workers were ordered to kill them…. In the end, as a result of the bison's decline and the encroachment of white European settlers, the Plains nations could no longer sustain their way of life.

7. ThinkSpeakListen

Summarize how the Transcontinental Railroad affected the lives of Americans.

Use Pronouns to Refer to Nouns

Noun	Pronoun
BALTIMORE & OHIO'S TOM THUMB — In 1830 <u>the first railroad</u> in the United States opened in Baltimore,	and <u>it</u> had just 21 kilometers (13 miles) of track.
<u>The Central Pacific Railroad Company</u> would begin in California, laying track east. <u>The Union Pacific Railroad Company</u> would start at the Missouri River, laying track west.	<u>They</u> would meet...in the middle.
There were <u>Irish, German, Chinese, and Swedish workers. Others were former enslaved laborers or ex-soldiers</u>....	<u>They</u> built tunnels through mountains, laid rail across deserts, and dug through snowstorms, mudslides, and avalanches.
People had expected <u>the transcontinental railroad</u> to be completed in 1876.	Instead, <u>it</u> was completed in 1869, seven years early.

8. ThinkSpeakListen

Explain how life was different for Americans before the Transcontinental Railroad. Use pronouns in your answer.

The Pony Express

The Pony Express was a mail delivery service...created to provide faster mail delivery to the West. Before then, the fastest way to transport mail was by stagecoach, which took twenty-five days.

A man named William Hepburn Russell...hired around eighty young men to carry mail by horseback from St. Joseph, Missouri, to Sacramento, California. There were around 190 relay stations at 16-kilometer (10-mile) intervals where a rider changed horses before proceeding on.

William Hepburn Russell

On April 3, 1860, the Pony Express began its first run. From the start, it was proclaimed a big success. The mail was delivered in ten days.

The Pony Express riders rode through blizzards and flooded rivers. Nothing interfered with delivering the mail.... Many riders became celebrities, the superstars of their day!

9. ThinkSpeakListen

Explain why the Pony Express was proclaimed a big success.

134

Writing to Sources

Informative/Explanatory

How did advancements in transportation change American society? After reading "The Open Road," "Dust Bowl Refugees," and "Building the Transcontinental Railroad," write a short essay that answers this question. Support your essay with evidence from each passage.

Research question

Research goal

Use of sources

Advancements in transportation helped to unite the American nation. As the result of new affordable automobiles, new interstate roads, and a transcontinental railroad, people began to travel more. As a result, Americans began to feel more connected to one another as citizens of one united country.

The writer introduces the topic and main ideas of the essay.

One major development that changed American society was the introduction of Henry Ford's Model T. Earlier cars had been very expensive, but this was affordable. According to "The Open Road," many people bought the Model T and "the need for paved roads, gas stations, and maps increased." The government built new interstate highways such as Route 66. New businesses developed along this route and people began to explore the country.

The writer develops the first main idea and supports it with evidence from the text.

The new network of roads and highways allowed people to explore their country. In some cases, people traveled long distances to start a whole new life. As "Dust Bowl Refugees" explains, this happened in the 1930s. The "Dust Bowl" was the name given to the area of the Midwest, including states like Oklahoma, which was hit by dust storms, or "black blizzards." As a result, people loaded up their cars and "hit the road and… hoped the open roads would lead to a better life."

The writer develops the second main idea and supports it with evidence from the text.

The transcontinental railroad was also a major advancement in transportation. Before the railroad was built to connect the East and West of the nation, travel across the country was long and difficult. It took four months by boat or wagon. However, when the transcontinental railroad was finished, it took only around a week to go from New York to San Francisco, according to "Building the Transcontinental Railroad." The trip was also much more affordable. Instead of $1,000, it cost $150. So, many more people traveled. Some even went west to settle new communities.

The writer develops the third main idea and supports it with evidence from the text.

The Oregon Trail

In 1803, President Thomas Jefferson purchased the Louisiana Territory from France. The Louisiana Purchase doubled the size of the United States, opening up the West for settlers. First, the region had to be mapped.

So, in 1804, the Lewis and Clark Expedition was tasked with the job of surveying the region and charting its rivers. The mission was a success, but their land route would prove too difficult for wagons.

The passes across the Rocky Mountains could be traveled only on foot, or on horseback. So, beginning in 1810, fur trappers and traders began carving a new trail out West.

Struggling farmers began to think about moving west, where the land was better and plentiful. So, the wave of settlers moving west began.

5

The people migrating west called themselves "emigrants" because they were leaving the states for unknown territories. Most of the people migrating kept diaries to record their journeys.

6

Narcissa Whitman

One woman who wrote a daily account of her journey on the Oregon Trail was Narcissa Whitman. In 1836, Whitman and her husband, Marcus, led a small expedition from New York to Oregon.

7

She described their daily routines and mishaps in her diary and letters…. Whitman recounts, "The present time in our journey is a very important one. The hunter brought us buffalo meat yesterday for the first time…. We have some for supper tonight…."

8

After traveling 3,200 kilometers (2,000 miles), the Whitmans had finally reached their new home in December 1836…. Soon after Narcissa Whitman made her trek on the Oregon Trail, others began to migrate there, too.

10. ThinkSpeakListen

What do you think life was like for emigrants on the Oregon Trail?

The travelers faced many hardships and dangers.... Sudden downpours, snowstorms, and hailstorms could divert the wagon train. Wagons would break down...and disease spread quickly among the people. Still, they pressed on...to reach Oregon safely and begin a new life there.

Then in 1848, gold was discovered in California. The lure of rich farmlands now changed to fields of gold. By 1850, more than 50,000 people traveled the Oregon Trail west. Instead of turning toward Oregon near the end of the trail, many turned to California.

By 1869, railroads connected California to the rest of the country and people moved west—using trains instead of wagons.... With new means of transportation, it was no longer needed.

Ezra Meeker

However, many pioneers kept the tales of the Oregon Trail alive. In 1852, pioneer Ezra Meeker wrote... a book about the many emigrants who traveled west to the trail's end.... Meeker worked to make the Oregon Trail a historic landmark, and today, it is.

11. ThinkSpeakListen

Describe the hardships faced by the travelers on the Oregon Trail.

Use Adjectives to Add Detail to Nouns

The people migrating west called themselves "emigrants" because they were leaving the states for <u>unknown</u> <u>territories</u>.

<u>Sudden</u> <u>downpours</u>, <u>snowstorms</u>, and <u>hailstorms</u> could divert the wagon train.

The lure of <u>rich</u> <u>farmlands</u> now changed to fields of gold.

Meeker worked to make the Oregon Trail a <u>historic</u> <u>landmark</u>, and today, it is.

12. ThinkSpeakListen

Why did people keep diaries of their travels on the Oregon Trail?

Oregon Trail Diary

Dear Diary,

In early September, we crossed the Blue Mountains of Oregon, which proved to be the most difficult part of our journey thus far!

The mountains were very steep... There was snow in some places, making the crossing even harder.

When the rope broke on the Smiths' wagon, we were terrified! We watched in horror as the wagon tumbled down the side of the mountain, but there was nothing to do but to continue walking. For two straight days it rained, and everyone was wet and cold. Finally, we made it to the other side....

Next week, we'll cross the Columbia River, and if all goes well, we should reach Oregon City a few weeks later. Pa plans to buy 250 acres of land, and then we'll build our new home. I'm eager to live in a house again and sleep in a real bed! And I can start school again.... I can't wait!

Your friend Sally
September 17, 1845

13. ThinkSpeakListen

What would it have been like to travel on the Oregon Trail in the 1800s?

Expand Sentences with Adverbs

Sentence	Adverb	Adjective Modified
...which proved to be the most difficult part of our journey thus far!	most	difficult
The mountains were very steep.	very	steep

Sentence	Adverb	Verb Modified
After traveling 3,200 kilometers (2,000 miles), the Whitmans had finally reached their new home in December 1836.	finally	reached
I'm eager to live in a house again and sleep in a real bed!	again	live

14. ThinkSpeakListen
Summarize the events of your day using adverbs to modify adjectives and verbs.

Essential Question

How do Earth's natural processes impact our lives?

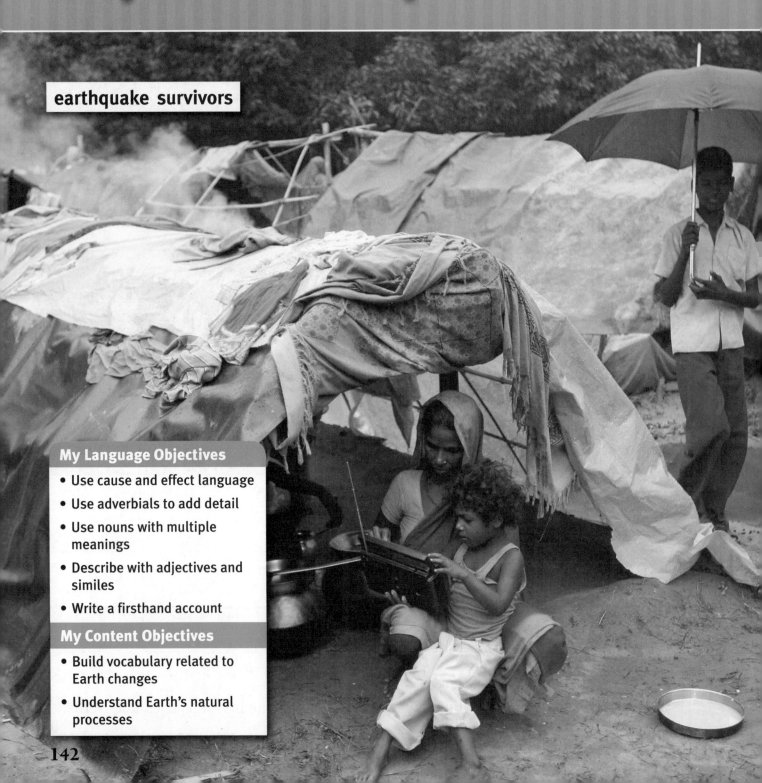

earthquake survivors

My Language Objectives

- Use cause and effect language
- Use adverbials to add detail
- Use nouns with multiple meanings
- Describe with adjectives and similes
- Write a firsthand account

My Content Objectives

- Build vocabulary related to Earth changes
- Understand Earth's natural processes

earthquake destruction

tsunami destruction

Earthquakes

by Kathy Furgang

1 An earthquake is a sudden movement or shift of Earth's crust.

tectonic plate

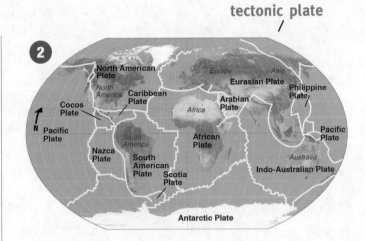

2 This thin outer layer is made of many interlocking pieces called tectonic plates....

3 When these plates shift or collide at their boundaries, an earthquake happens.

4 Earth's surface rumbles and shakes as the energy is released....

1. ThinkSpeakListen

Explain how an earthquake occurs.

Use Cause-and-Effect Language

Cause	Effect

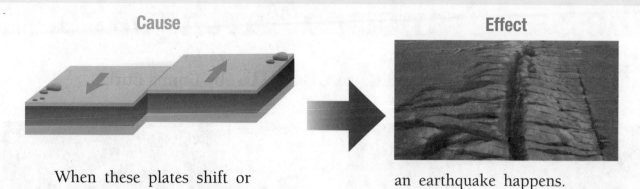

When these plates shift or collide at their boundaries,

an earthquake happens.

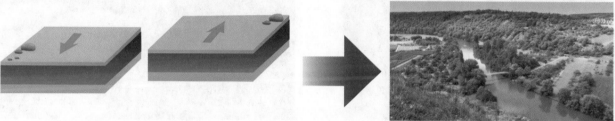

As plates move apart,

valleys, rivers, and even oceans can form.

The Himalayan mountain range in Asia, for example, was formed when the Indo-Australian and Eurasian plates came together. The plates collided and pushed upward, slowly forming the mighty mountain range over the last ten million years.

2. ThinkSpeakListen
Describe a cause and effect to your partner.

The San Francisco Earthquake, 1906: An Eyewitness Account by Emma Burke

It was 5:13 a.m., and my husband had arisen and lit the gas stove, and put on the water to heat.... We were in a fourth-story apartment flat....

The shock came, and hurled my bed against an opposite wall. I sprang up, and, holding firmly to the foot-board managed to keep on my feet to the door....

We braced ourselves in the doorway, clinging to the casing. Our son appeared across the reception room....

It grew constantly worse, the noise deafening; the crash of dishes, falling pictures, the rattle of the flat tin roof....

5

The floor moved like short, choppy waves of the sea, crisscrossed by a tide as mighty as themselves....

6

My husband told me to dress quickly and get down our tortuous stairs to the street....

7

After a half-hour we came up to our flat.... I walked over the remains of my choicest china, porcelain, and cut-glass, without a feeling of regret or a sigh or tear....

8

Human life seemed the only thing worth consideration.

3. ThinkSpeakListen

Describe what happened during the earthquake.

Tsunami!

A tsunami can be one huge ocean wave…traveling hundreds of miles an hour. However, on the surface, the waves appear small and insignificant, so passing ships don't notice them.

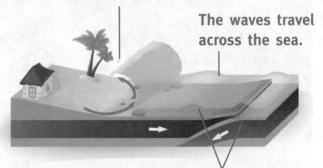

The tsunami hits the coast.

The waves travel across the sea.

A tsunami starts during an earthquake.

As they move toward land, they slow down and grow taller and taller. Some waves measure more than 70 feet high!

When a tsunami hits land, it can cause unbelievable destruction. People, homes, and trees are picked up and tossed around. Those lucky enough to survive face nearly impossible challenges. Their homes and neighborhoods may have disappeared. Family members and friends may have died.

4. ThinkSpeakListen

Describe what happens when a tsunami hits land.

Use Adverbials to Add Detail

Sentence with an Adverbial Phrase	Question the Adverbial Phrase Answers
As plates move apart, valleys, rivers, and even oceans can form. 	**When** can valleys, rivers, and oceans form?
It grew **constantly** worse, the noise deafening; the crash of dishes, falling pictures, the rattle of the flat tin roof. 	**How** did the earthquake grow worse?
In the deep ocean, these waves move incredibly fast. 	**Where** do the tsunami waves move incredibly fast?

5. ThinkSpeakListen
Summarize what you learned about tsunamis.

Volcanoes by Brett Kelly

Earth's Layers

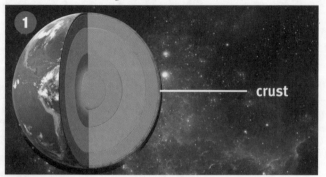

Earth is made up of four different layers: the crust, the mantle, the outer core, and the inner core.... The crust is formed from giant slabs, or plates, of rock. These plates fit together like pieces in a jigsaw puzzle. Together they float on another layer called the mantle....

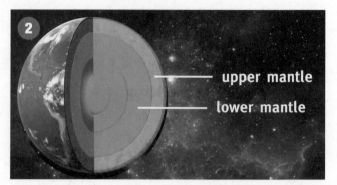

The upper mantle is composed of cold, dense rock. The lower mantle is made of partially molten rock that flows....

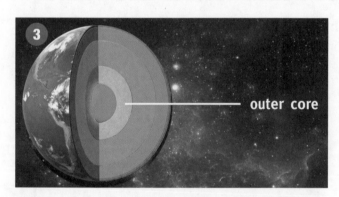

The next layer is Earth's outer core, which is made up of very hot liquid (molten) lava....

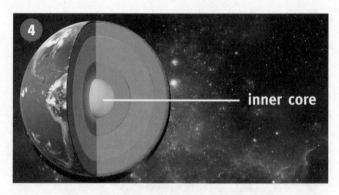

The inner core...is a solid ball made of metals.

How Does a Volcano Happen?

Cause	Effect
The heat and pressure inside Earth are so great…	that solid rock is constantly melting and forming liquid magma.
Because the liquid magma is lighter than solid rock,	the magma rises and the solid rock sinks. Some magma cools as it rises, becoming solid rock and sinking again. Other magma remains liquid and collects in underground chambers.
When the heat and pressure build in these chambers,	the magma is pushed through cracks in Earth's surface. The result is a volcanic eruption.

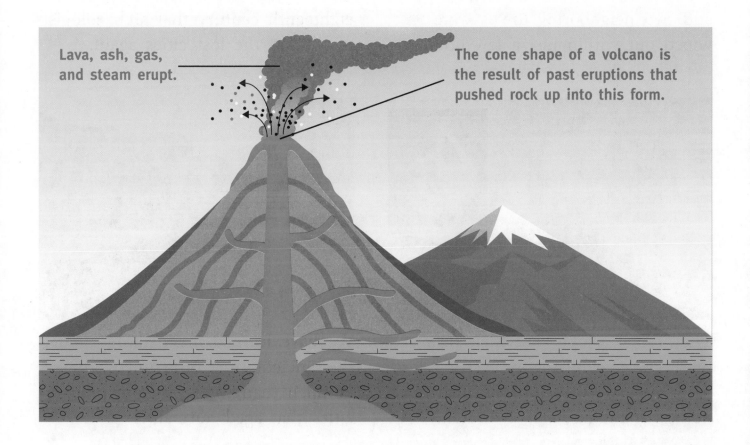

Lava, ash, gas, and steam erupt.

The cone shape of a volcano is the result of past eruptions that pushed rock up into this form.

6. ThinkSpeakListen

Describe what happens when pressure builds in a volcano's magma chamber.

Famous Eruptions

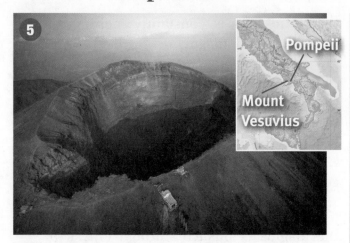

The most famous volcanic eruption in history occurred at Mount Vesuvius in Italy in 79 CE. Pompeii and two neighboring towns were wiped out within just a few hours....

The eruption sealed the region as if in a time capsule for more than 1,700 years. It wasn't until the eighteenth century that archaeologists uncovered the lost cities again.

They found people and their pets preserved in white, ashy casts. Also preserved were the remains of homes, fountains, and a theater....

We have learned much more about this ancient time from uncovering Pompeii than we have from other cities that aged normally.

7. ThinkSpeakListen

Why was the discovery of Pompeii so important?

Use Nouns with Multiple Meanings

Noun	Meaning in "Volcanoes"	Everyday Meanings	
crust	 the outer layer of Earth	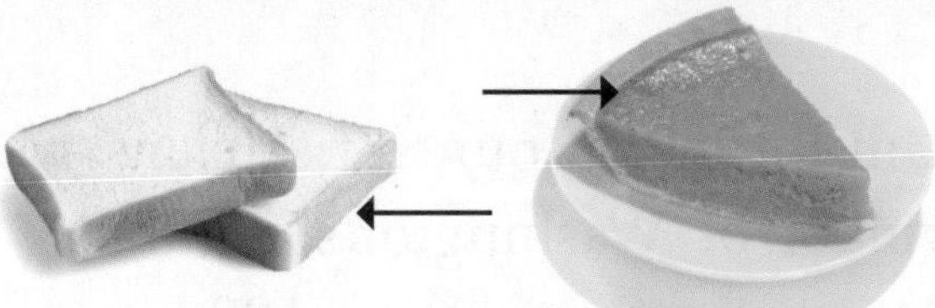 the outer portion of bread or pie	
core	 the innermost part of Earth	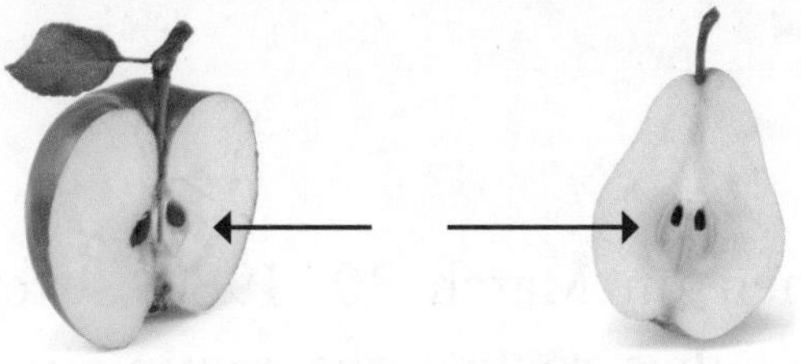 the innermost part of some fruit	
cast	 an object made from a mold	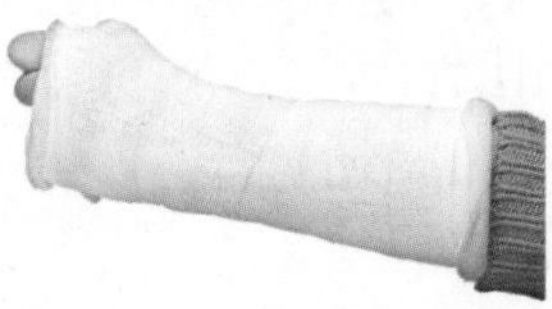 a hard bandage to protect bones	 the people in a play or movie
plates	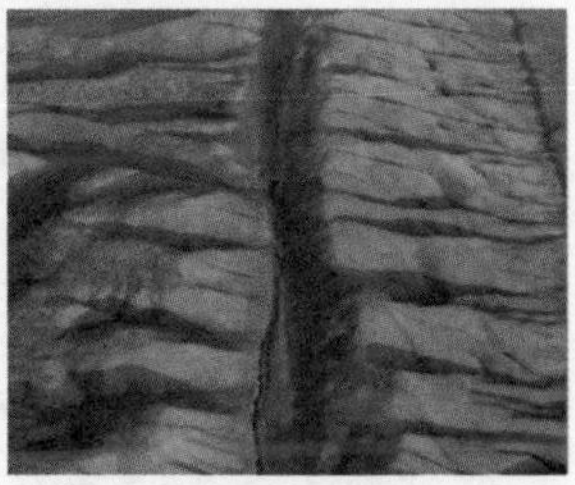 slabs of interlocking rock that make up Earth's crust	 dishes	

8. ThinkSpeakListen

Choose one of the words in the chart above. What do its different meanings have in common?

153

The Mount St. Helens Volcano

Until 1980, Mount St. Helens was a symbol of Washington's natural beauty.... For more than 100 years, the volcano was peaceful.

Then on March 20, 1980, several earthquakes rocked the mountain. Many people were surprised. However, geologists who had been studying the volcano for years weren't surprised at all....

On the morning of May 18, 1980, Mount St. Helens erupted with great force. Clouds of smoke, steam, and ash filled the air. The sky was as dark as night. The eruption continued for hours, destroying 230 square miles. Plant and animal habitats on the mountain were disrupted and devastated, and 57 people died.

9. ThinkSpeakListen

Summarize what happened after Mount St. Helens erupted on May 18, 1980.

Research and Writing

Research Topic

Type of Writing

Prompt

<u>Research an Earth change event in the recent or distant past. Present a fictional, firsthand account of what you saw, heard, and felt during and after the event.</u>

My Pre-Search Results

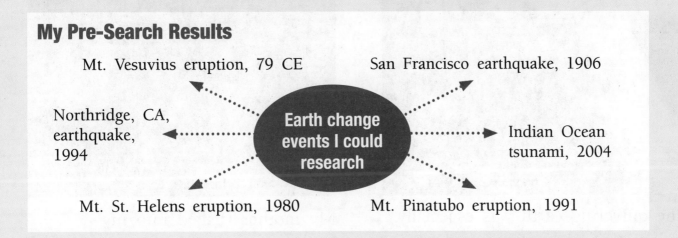

Mt. Vesuvius eruption, 79 CE

San Francisco earthquake, 1906

Northridge, CA, earthquake, 1994

Earth change events I could research

Indian Ocean tsunami, 2004

Mt. St. Helens eruption, 1980

Mt. Pinatubo eruption, 1991

My Research Findings

Event: San Francisco Earthquake, 1906	
Where did it happen?	in and around San Francisco, CA, along the San Andreas fault
When did it happen?	April 18, 1906
What happened during the earthquake?	• The ground shook for 45 to 60 seconds. • More than 3,000 people died. • 225,000 people became homeless. • 28,000 buildings were destroyed. • After the earthquake, bad fires broke out. • Many people had to live in tents or housing camps. • People stood in long lines for food.

Mount Vesuvius, 79 CE:
Letter from Pliny the Younger

The quivering earth was especially violent that night. It not only shook, but also overturned everything around us.

My mother rushed into my bedroom.... We sat down in the open area of the house, in a small space between the buildings and the sea....

Though it was now morning, the light was still dim. The buildings all around us tottered.... there was no remaining ground that was not in danger. We therefore decided to leave our town....

Above, a black and dreadful cloud, broken with rapid, zigzag flashes, revealed behind it variously shaped masses of flame. The bigger flames were like sheet-lightning....

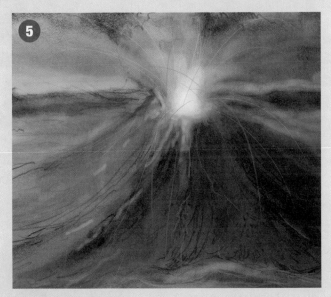

5

Soon afterwards, the cloud began to lower and cover the sea....

6

My mother now begged, urged, and even commanded me to make my escape.... She said her age and weight made the journey impossible....

7

But I absolutely refused to leave her. I took her by the hand, and forced her to go with me....

10. ThinkSpeakListen

Explain why Pliny and his mother decided to leave town.

The ashes now began to fall upon us.... I looked back. A dense dark mist seemed to be following us. It spread itself over the country like a cloud....

Night came upon us.... We heard the shrieks of women, the screams of children, and the shouts of men....

The sky now grew rather lighter, which we imagined to be an approaching burst of flames.... the fire fell at a distance from us. Then again we were immersed in thick darkness.

A heavy shower of ashes rained upon us. From time to time, we had to stand up to shake off the ashes or be crushed by the weight of them.... I believed I was dying with the whole world.

11. ThinkSpeakListen

Why did Pliny believe he was "dying with the whole world"?

Describe with Adjectives and Similes

Above, a <u>black</u> and <u>dreadful</u> cloud, broken with <u>rapid, zigzag</u> flashes…

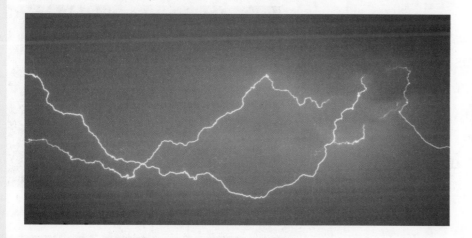

The <u>bigger</u> flames were <u>like sheet-lightning</u>…

A <u>dense dark</u> mist seemed to be following us. It spread itself over the country <u>like a cloud</u>.…

12. ThinkSpeakListen

Look at the paintings and photographs. Describe them using adjectives and similes.

Escape from Pompeii

It is August 24, 79 CE. Marcus and his father are at their fish stall in the forum, Pompeii's busy marketplace.... They have been working since dawn....

stall

Suddenly, around noon, there is a fiery blast from Mount Vesuvius, causing the ground to tremble! A huge, dark cloud forms above the mountain, and the wind blows it toward Pompeii. It is dark as night, and hot ash pours down.

"Father, what is happening?" Marcus shouts in fear.

"It is a fire blast from the mountain!" replies his father. "We must flee or we will surely perish!"

"What about all our fish?" asks Marcus.

"Leave everything and come quickly!"

forum

13. ThinkSpeakListen

How is "Escape from Pompeii" similar to "Mount Vesuvius, 79 CE"? How is it different?

Research and Writing

Prompt

Research an Earth change event in the recent or distant past. Present a fictional, firsthand account of what you saw, heard, and felt during and after the event.

Research Topic

Type of Writing

Sample Planning Guide

Firsthand Account Planning Guide	
Title: "The Day San Francisco Trembled"	
Characters	Narrator: Tom, a twelve-year-old boy Tom's father
Setting	Sacramento Street, in San Francisco
Events	Beginning: Tom is sleeping. The earthquake begins.
	Middle: Tom and his father run out to the street.
	End: Tom watches his building topple.

Sample Firsthand Account

The vibrations woke me up. My bed was shaking and the walls were groaning like someone in pain. My father appeared in the doorway. "Tom, we have to get out!" he yelled above the loud roar.

We flew down the stairs and pushed our way through the front door. Frantic people were screaming in terror. My father held my hand firmly. "We can't stay here," he said. "It's too dangerous."

Just then, we heard a deafening crash. Our tall brick building toppled to the ground like toy blocks. We stared at the rubble. Then we stared at each other. Our life was never going to be the same again.

Essential Question

How does access to resources influence people's lives?

dust storm

My Language Objectives

- Use the language of sequence
- Use context clues to understand foreign terms
- Use the language of cause and effect
- Describe with similes and metaphors
- Write an informative essay

My Content Objectives

- Build vocabulary related to resources, business, and population
- Understand how access to resources affects individuals and society

162

farmworkers

oil drill

Seattle: Up and Down—and Up Again

by Alexandra Hanson-Harding

Today, Seattle is famous for its high-tech companies, such as Microsoft and Amazon. But when Seattle was established in the 1850s, its economy was supported by a lumber mill....

When the railroads arrived in the 1880s, Seattle's population grew quickly. In the first half of 1889, Seattle gained 1,000 new residents every month....

In the years that followed, Seattle became a "boom or bust" town. In the 1890s, a nationwide depression crippled Seattle's economy.

Then, in 1897, the Klondike Gold Rush began. Seattle became the main supplier for the thousands of miners who came to Alaska. Seattle was a "boom" town once again.

1. ThinkSpeakListen

Summarize the changes that Seattle's economy went through from the 1850s to the 1890s.

Use the Language of Sequence

View from Downtown Seattle, Washington

Sentence	Word or Phrase That Indicates Sequence
Today, Seattle is famous for its high-tech companies, such as Microsoft and Amazon.	**Today**
When the railroads arrived in the 1880s, Seattle's population grew quickly.	**When the railroads arrived in the 1880s**
In the years that followed, Seattle became a "boom or bust" town.	**In the years that followed**
In the 1890s, a nationwide depression crippled Seattle's economy.	**In the 1890s**
Then, in 1897, the Klondike Gold Rush began.	**Then, in 1897**

2. ThinkSpeakListen
Why is it important for a writer to use the language of sequence? What might happen if a writer does not use this type of language?

César:

¡Sí, Se Puede! Yes, We Can!

Poems by Carmen T. Bernier-Grand

Who Could Tell?

¡Híjole!
Who could tell?

Who could tell
that Cesario Estrada Chávez
the shy American
wearing a checkered shirt,
walking with a cane to ease his back
from the burden of the fields,
could organize so many people
to march for *La Causa*, The Cause?

Who could tell
that he with a soft *pan dulce* voice,
hair the color of mesquite,
and downcast, Aztec eyes,
would have the courage to speak up
for the *campesinos*
to get better pay,
better housing,
better health?

¡Híjole!
Who could tell?

Green Gold

Lechuguero,
a lettuce thinner,
a man, a woman, or a child
who pulls off smaller plants
to make room for bigger plants—
the *patrón's* green gold.

Row after row
César walked.
Stooped over, twisted,
clawing at the *chuga*
with *el cortito*,
a short-handed hoe.

No boots, just shoes
sinking in mud,
clay clinging to the soles.

Every day swathed in scarves
covering his nose and mouth.
Trying not to breathe,
trying not to swallow
the smelly spray blowing on him.

3. ThinkSpeakListen

Compare the moods of these two poems about César Chávez.

Dolores Huerta

Labor leader, community organizer, and champion of farmworkers' rights, Dolores Huerta has devoted her life to improving the lives of those around her.

Dolores Huerta

Huerta's father was a miner and farmworker who later became an activist and state politician. Her mother owned a restaurant and hotel in a California migrant worker community…. Dolores Huerta saw firsthand that employment as a migrant worker meant low pay and little dignity. She understood the difficulties they faced….

In the 1960s, Huerta co-founded the National Farm Workers Association with César Chávez. This organization, now called the United Farm Workers, gave them the voice they needed to fight for equality.

César Chávez

4. ThinkSpeakListen

Explain why Dolores Huerta's work in the 1960s was important.

Use Context Clues to Understand Foreign Terms

Word (poem)	Context Clues and Our Definition
pan dulce ("Who Could Tell?")	"soft" "voice" |_____| *pleasant*
	Revised definition using references: *sweet bread*

Word (poem)	Context Clues and Our Definition
campesinos ("Who Could Tell?")	"to get better pay"	*workers*
	Revised definition using references: *farmworkers*

Word (poem)	Context Clues and Our Definition
patrón's ("Green Gold")	"plants" "green gold" |_____| *a rich farm owner*
	Revised definition using references: *boss* or *employer*

5. ThinkSpeakListen

Why did the poet choose to use foreign words in her poems?

Natural Resources and Workers

by Alexandra Hanson-Harding

In the 1700s, Spanish priests came to California to start missions, which functioned as both religious and farming centers....

Native Americans were forced to work in the fields under poor conditions. The missions also set up Native American settlements close to their farms so that they could supervise their workers....

Gold was discovered in California in 1848, and in 1849 the rush for gold began.... As the population in California grew, so did the need for food. As a result, the agricultural industry continued to grow....

In the early 1860s, the United States hired Chinese workers to help build the Transcontinental Railroad. When it was completed in 1869, these workers flocked to California....

6. ThinkSpeakListen

Recount the different groups of people mentioned so far in the text, and what each group did.

5

By 1930, the Great Depression, a period of economic hardship that lasted from 1929 to the early 1940s, forced prices for farm goods to drop. As a result, workers' wages dropped, too.

6

Many European American farmers, fleeing the severe droughts of the Midwest, began searching for jobs in California.... They were called migrant workers. They struggled to survive because there were too many migrant workers and not enough jobs.

7

In the 1940s, World War II began. During those years, the U.S. government forced California's Japanese Americans into "Relocation Camps" such as Manzanar, deep in California's desert.

8

They were forced into these camps because the United States was at war with Japan and considered Japanese Americans as potential enemies. As a result, many Japanese Americans had their homes and farming businesses taken from them.

During the war, new factory jobs opened up, so many farmworkers left the fields for factory jobs that paid better.

But farms still needed workers. The United States started the *Braceros* (manual laborers) program. It gave Mexicans limited visas to work in California's fields, but it prevented them from becoming citizens....

In recent years, California has faced a shortage of farmworkers. Still, few American citizens want to work the state's farms because of the low pay for hard work.

So some farm owners rely on undocumented immigrants to harvest their crops. The need for farmworkers, and the debate about legal immigration, is often in the news.

7. ThinkSpeakListen

Recount the events and circumstances that have affected the population of farmworkers in California.

Use the Language of Cause and Effect

> cause
> As the population in California grew, so did the need for food. **As a result**, the
> effect
> agricultural industry continued to grow.

> effect   cause
> They struggled to survive **because** there were too many migrant workers and not
> enough jobs.

> effect   cause
> They were forced into these camps **because** the United States was at war with
> Japan and considered Japanese Americans as potential enemies.

> cause
> By 1930, the Great Depression…forced prices for farm goods to drop. **As a result**,
> effect
> workers' wages dropped, too.

> cause   effect
> During the war, new factory jobs opened up, **so** many farmworkers left the fields
> for factory jobs that paid better.

8. ThinkSpeakListen

Explain how sentences that use "As a result" and "so" should be arranged, and how sentences using "because" should be arranged differently.

John Henry

John Henry's parents knew nothing about agriculture, but they knew how to cultivate a powerful boy.... When John Henry grew up, he became a steel driver for the railroad...

One year when the railroad was constructing a tunnel, a salesman showed up and introduced a newly manufactured machine. It was a steam drill. The salesman bragged that it could outwork any man.

"It can't outwork mighty John Henry," replied the railroad boss, and so a contest between John Henry and the machine was arranged....

At first, the machine worked faster than John Henry, so John Henry grabbed another hammer and worked with both arms. Without intermission, he hammered. The ground trembled until the machine overheated and stopped.

John Henry strode out of the tunnel with his hammers held high in triumph.

9. ThinkSpeakListen
Describe both John Henry and the salesman. What are their character traits?

Research and Writing

Prompt

"Seattle: Up and Down—and Up Again" describes how Seattle was affected by a gold rush in the 1800s. Research another city that was affected by a gold rush, and write an informative report about how the gold rush affected that city.

Background Knowledge

Research Question

Research Goal

Guiding Question 1:
How did the population of San Francisco change during the gold rush?

- The population grew by over 35,000.
- Many Chinese immigrants settled there.

Guiding Question 2:
How did the gold rush affect the economy of the area?

- New businesses were created, such as Levi Strauss & Co. and the Ghirardelli Chocolate Company.
- New banks formed, such as Wells Fargo and the Bank of California.
- Wealthy business owners built mansions in the Nob Hill area.

Guiding Question 3:
How did the gold rush affect government and society?

- Crime and corruption in government increased.
- San Francisco was divided into two counties.

Out of the Dust

by Karen Hesse

Fields of Flashing Light

I heard the wind rise,
and stumbled from my bed,
down the stairs,
out the front door,
into the yard.
The night sky kept flashing,
lightning danced down on its spindly legs....

While Ma and Daddy slept,
the dust came,
tearing up fields where the winter wheat,
set for harvest in June,
stood helpless.
I watched the plants,
surviving after so much drought and so much
  wind,
I watched them fry,
or
flatten,
or blow away,
like bits of cast-off rags.

It wasn't until the dust turned toward the
    house,
like a fired locomotive,
and I fled,
barefoot and breathless, back inside,
it wasn't until the dust
hissed against the windows,
until it ratcheted the roof,
that Daddy woke.

He ran into the storm,
his overalls half-hooked over his union suit.
"Daddy!" I called. "You can't stop dust."

Ma told me to
cover the beds,
push the scatter rugs against the doors,
dampen the rags around the windows.
Wiping dust out of everything,
she made coffee and biscuits,
waiting for Daddy to come in.

10. ThinkSpeakListen
Summarize what has happened so far in this narrative poem.

Sometime after four,
rubbing low on her back,
Ma sank down into a chair at the kitchen
    table
and covered her face.
Daddy didn't come back for hours,
not
until the temperature dropped so low,
it brought snow.

Ma and I sighed, grateful,
staring out at the dirty flakes,
but our relief didn't last.
The wind snatched that snow right off the
    fields,
leaving behind a sea of dust,
waves and
waves and
waves of
dust,
rippling across our yard....

March 1934

11. ThinkSpeakListen

What do you think Ma is feeling in this poem? State your opinion, and be sure
to point to evidence in the text.

Describe with Similes and Metaphors

Similes

I watched the plants,
…blow away,
like bits of cast-off rags.

It wasn't until the dust turned toward the house,
like a fired locomotive…

Metaphors

The night sky kept flashing,
lightning danced down on its **spindly legs**.

The wind snatched that snow right off the fields,
leaving behind a **sea of dust**.

12. ThinkSpeakListen

Explain how similes and metaphors can help a writer express ideas to the reader.

Dust Storm Days

Mother stands on the porch and stares at the darkening horizon with despair.... An enormous black cloud is rolling toward us. It's time to prepare for another dust storm!...

My sister and I scurry around the barnyard rounding up chickens. The gritty air tears at our faces. Once the chickens are in their coop, we dash back to the house....

Father has been in the barn checking on our mare. When he returns, he is covered with dust and is holding a damp cloth to his mouth so he can breathe....

Damage caused by this dust storm can be repaired, but I'm not sure my family has the forbearance to remain here. Mother swears it's time to move to California.... But there's no work for us there. Still, our crops are devastated, and the dust clogs our lungs and wears out our spirit. I wonder—are we strong enough to survive these dust storm days?

13. ThinkSpeakListen
Explain the difficult decision the family faces, and the reasons that the decision is difficult.

Research and Writing

Prompt

"Seattle: Up and Down—and Up Again" describes how Seattle was affected by a gold rush in the 1800s. Research another city that was affected by a gold rush, and write an informative report about how the gold rush affected that city.

Background Knowledge

Research Subject

Research Goal

Sample Essay

The California Gold Rush of the 1840s and 1850s affected many communities in northern California, as thousands of people flocked to the region in search of gold. One of these communities was San Francisco. During the gold rush, the population of San Francisco increased by over 35,000. This growth brought with it both a boom in the economy and drastic changes to the society of the city.

> The introduction clearly presents the essay's main topic.

As the population of San Francisco grew, so did its economy. New businesses were created, including the Ghirardelli Chocolate Company and Levi Strauss & Co., which sold clothing. Banks were also formed, such as Wells Fargo and the Bank of California. With this economic development came very wealthy residents, and many mansions were built in the Nob Hill area.

The growth in population also caused the society of San Francisco to change. The city became more culturally diverse, as new Chinese immigrants became a significant part of the community. Unfortunately, the city's growth also led to government corruption and crime, and a Committee of Vigilance was organized to try to solve these problems.

> The body paragraphs develop the topic with facts and concrete details related to the topic.

Eventually, the California state government decided to split San Francisco into two separate counties. The northern half became modern-day San Francisco, which has continued to grow economically and culturally as the large, diverse community that it is today.

> The concluding paragraph follows from the information presented and brings the essay to a close.

Essential Question

Where do scientific discoveries lead us?

lightning over a field

My Language Objectives

- Use plural nouns
- Use complete sentences
- Use apostrophes to form possessive nouns
- Expand sentences with prepositional phrases
- Write an opinion essay

My Content Objectives

- Build vocabulary related to electricity discoveries
- Understand important scientific developments in electricity

a train powered by electricity

mirrors that capture energy from the sun

Power Restored in India by Abby Lieberman

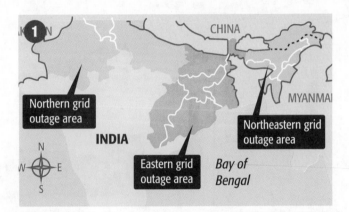

On July 30, India's northern electric grid failed.... The failure of three national power grids plunged half the country into darkness.

An electric grid is a network of power stations, fuel, and power lines that work together to deliver electricity.

Officials believe that...the grids were unable to produce the amount of energy that residents were using. "If they overdraw, this is the result," said India's power minister....

Now, many are wondering whether the country needs to work harder to improve its infrastructure, or basic facilities.

1. ThinkSpeakListen

Summarize the key facts about the power outage in India.

Use Plural Nouns

Singular Noun	+ "s"	Plural Noun
Grid	Grid + s	The failure of three national power <u>grids</u> plunged half the country into darkness.
Official	Official + s	<u>Officials</u> believe that…the grids were unable to produce the amount of energy that <u>residents</u> were using.
Resident	Resident + s	
Station	Station + s	An electric grid is a network of power <u>stations</u>, fuel, and power lines that work together to deliver electricity.

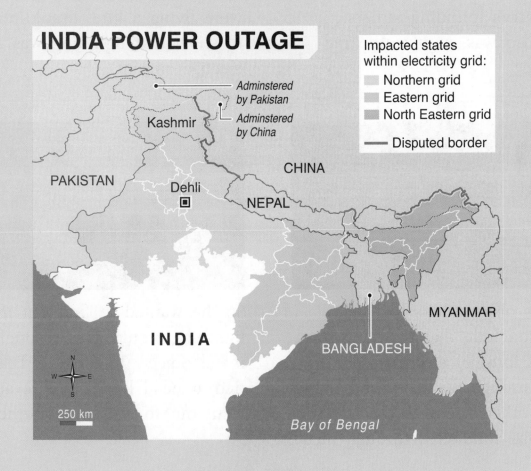

INDIA POWER OUTAGE

Impacted states within electricity grid:
- Northern grid
- Eastern grid
- North Eastern grid
- Disputed border

Adminstered by Pakistan
Adminstered by China
Kashmir
PAKISTAN
CHINA
Dehli
NEPAL
INDIA
MYANMAR
BANGLADESH
Bay of Bengal
250 km

2. ThinkSpeakListen

Describe the cause and effects of the blackout in India.

Benjamin Franklin: The Dawn of Electrical Technology
by Laura McDonald

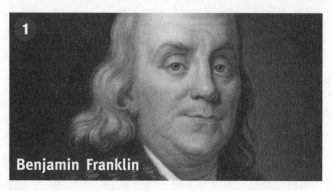

Benjamin Franklin

Benjamin Franklin was one of the most influential thinkers of the eighteenth century. He was one of our country's founding fathers.... But he also was an inventor and scientist....

One stormy day in June 1752, Franklin stood in the doorway of a shed with his son William. They were flying a kite. Franklin wanted to show that lightning was a type of electric current....

Franklin's observations had led him to conclude that lightning was a natural form of electricity. He learned through his work and the work of other scientists that electric energy was conducted through metal.

So, he wanted to find out if lightning would pass through a metal object. To do this, Franklin tied a metal key to a kite and went out to test his hypothesis.

5

Joseph Priestley

An account of this famous event was written by scientist Joseph Priestley...: *"He [Franklin] immediately presented his knuckle to the key, and...he perceived a very evident electric spark...."*

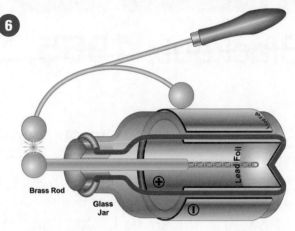

6

Brass Rod
Glass Jar
Lead Foil

Franklin collected "electric fire" in a Leyden (LY-den) jar. A Leyden jar is a glass jar with a glass layer sandwiched between two metal layers. Electrons build up on the metal layers. When a conductor connects the two metal layers, the jar produces an electric spark....

7

By connecting Leyden jars together, he would invent an early type of battery. Franklin also invented the lightning rod.... Lightning rods have saved many people's homes and lives....

8

Franklin was a curious and intelligent man. He helped to form the first public library and the first fire department in Pennsylvania. Franklin also helped to write the Declaration of Independence....

3. ThinkSpeakListen

Summarize Benjamin Franklin's discoveries. Which one do you think was most important?

Blackout, 1965

When the power went out during my last stay at Granddad's, I was miserable. After all, my cell phone needed charging....

"Aw, it's not so bad," he said. "You should have been in New York City in 1965. Now that was a real blackout!

"Of course, the elevators in my office building weren't working," Granddad said, "so my coworkers and I inched our way down sixteen flights of stairs using candles. The subways were out, too, so we ate in a restaurant by candlelight and then snagged places to sleep in a hotel lobby. The next day I found out that some people had been stuck in subway cars. Others had been trapped in elevators in the Empire State Building!"...

"Well, maybe this blackout isn't so bad," I said. "At least we're not stuck in an elevator!" Just as I spoke, the lights flickered on and the air conditioner resumed its familiar humming.

4. ThinkSpeakListen

What would you do during a blackout without any lights or electricity?

Use Complete Sentences

Subject +		Verb =	Complete Sentence
	Franklin	wanted	**Franklin wanted** to show that lightning was a type of electric current.
	He	learned	**He learned** through his work... that electric energy was conducted through metal.

Subject +		Verb =	Complete Sentence
	Franklin	tied	**Franklin tied** a metal key to a kite.
	He	helped	**He helped** to form the first public library and the first fire department in Pennsylvania.

5. ThinkSpeakListen

Describe some of Ben Franklin's other interests and achievements in addition to discovering electricity.

The Power of Electricity

by Kathy Furgang

In today's world, most people depend...on electricity for light and heat. They need it to cook and clean.... They use it to travel from place to place. They use it to communicate....

But what is electricity?... The answer is in the science of atoms. All matter—everything in the universe—is made of tiny building blocks called atoms....

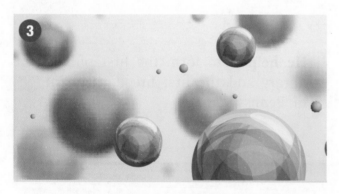

All atoms are made up of particles. Positively charged particles are called *protons*. Particles with no charge are called *neutrons*. Negatively charged particles are called *electrons*.... Electricity is the movement, or flow, of electrons from atom to atom....

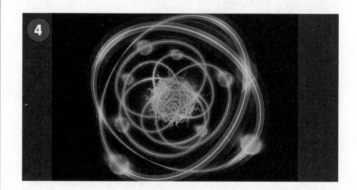

There are two types of electricity. When the electric charge is stationary, or not moving, the result is static electricity....

When an electric charge is moving through matter, the result is current electricity....

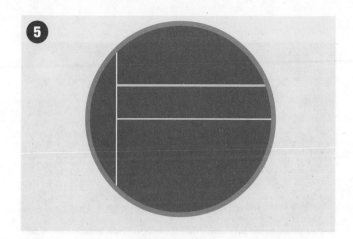

5 There are two types of currents. When the electrons always flow in the same direction, it is called direct current, or DC. Flashlights and cell phones all use batteries and DC power....

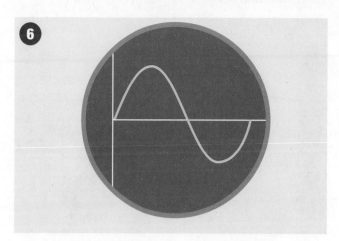

6 An alternating current, or AC, reverses, or alternates, direction fifty or sixty times per second. Everything that plugs into an outlet uses AC power. Alternating current is used when high-power voltages are required....

7 Where does the electricity that people consume come from? Energy can be converted, or changed, from one form to another. That means stored or mechanical energy can be converted to electric energy....

United States transmission grid
Source: FEMA

8 In the United States, electricity starts at power plants and enters a complex power grid. This grid can be compared to a network of roads.... Control centers act like traffic cops, making sure the electricity goes where it is needed.

6. ThinkSpeakListen

Describe the two types of currents and explain how they work.

Eventually, electricity makes its way through the network of power lines to its destination—the outlets in homes and businesses. Most of the work to control the flow of electricity is done automatically by computers....

When a computer malfunctions, or breaks, transmission is obstructed, or blocked. The result is a blackout, where the electric power fails in a region....

Many people think better technologies....would help conserve energy resources.... Scientists are also developing alternative energy sources such as renewable wind and solar power.

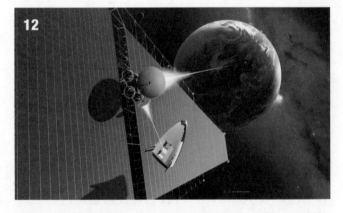

The National Aeronautics and Space Administration (NASA) has plans to launch a series of mirrors into space to collect energy from the sun and redirect it to Earth. In the future, NASA may also use kites to capture the wind's energy....

7. ThinkSpeakListen

Explain how a power grid delivers electricity to homes and businesses.

Use Apostrophes to Form Possessive Nouns

Text	Possessive Noun	Sentence with Possessive Noun
Restoring Power to India	**India's** = of or belonging to India	On July 30, **India's** northern electric grid failed.
Benjamin Franklin: The Dawn of Electrical Technology	**Franklin's** = of or belonging to Franklin	**Franklin's** observations had led him to conclude that lightning was a natural form of electricity.
The Power of Electricity	**today's** = of or belonging to today	In **today's** world, most people depend on electricity...for light and heat.
	wind's = of or belonging to the wind	In the future, NASA may also use kites to capture the **wind's** energy....

8. ThinkSpeakListen

What do you think are the most important discoveries scientists have made about electricity?

The Hoover Dam

Electricity is essential to our lives. We use it to charge our phones, operate our kitchen appliances, and light our streets. Where does all this electricity come from? Much of it comes from power plants that run on fossil or nuclear fuel. Some is generated by solar or wind power. And some of it comes from hydroelectric plants that harness the power of water. One of the largest hydroelectric plants in the country is housed at the base of Hoover Dam.

Built in the 1930s, Hoover Dam is a huge concrete structure that spans the Colorado River between Arizona and Nevada. The dam was built to control the flow of the river and provide water to the barren desert. It was also built to produce electricity.

When the Colorado River was dammed, a lake called Lake Mead was created. The water from Lake Mead is used to generate electricity.

9. ThinkSpeakListen

Summarize the main sources of electricity.

Research and Writing

Informative/Explanatory

Research one invention or discovery that has affected the way we power our lives. In an opinion essay, explain why you think this invention or discovery has had the greatest impact on the way we use electricity. Make sure to defend your opinion with reasons and evidence.

Research you will do

Essay you will write

Evidence you will use

Opinion and Reasons Chart	
What is my topic?	the battery
What is my opinion about my topic?	The invention of the battery has had the greatest impact on how we power our lives.

What reasons support my opinion about this topic?	• Mobile technology is crucial to the lives of many people today:
	  ▶ cell phones
	  ▶ portable computers
	• Without batteries, mobile technology would not be possible.

What is my thesis or belief statement?	By making mobile technology possible, the battery is the invention that has had the greatest impact on how we power our lives today.

Nikola Tesla: Electrifying Inventor

by Alexandra Hanson-Harding

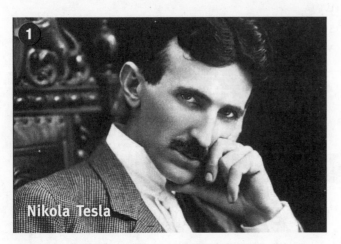

Nikola Tesla

Nikola Tesla was...one of the most brilliant scientists who ever lived....

Scientists call Tesla "the father of the electric age".... Yet his work has been left off the pages of most history books.

Thomas Edison

One reason for this was because Tesla competed throughout his career with fellow inventor Thomas Edison. The two were as different as night and day. Edison....was always thinking of ways to make money from his inventions.

Tesla, on the other hand, was devoted to science—not money. He valued what his inventions could do for the world, not his bank account....

Edison's ideas were practical—simple and useful but not always the most efficient or advanced. Tesla's vision was more ambitious....

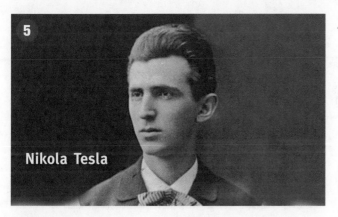

Nikola Tesla

Tesla was born in what is now Croatia to Serbian parents in 1856.... He did not focus...on science until he prepared to come to the United States at the age of twenty-eight.

Tesla started out working for...Edison when he immigrated...in 1884.

Edison had developed direct current (DC) transmission—a way of sending electricity over long distances.... But DC power was not efficient. It needed power stations every two miles. It required vast amounts of copper wiring.

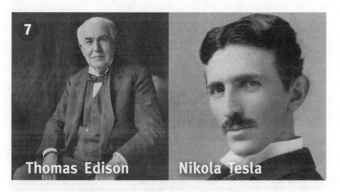

Thomas Edison   Nikola Tesla

Edison offered Tesla $50,000 if he could improve the way energy was transmitted. But after Tesla presented his improvements to Edison, Edison said that he had been joking about the $50,000. Furious, Tesla quit. The two became competitors.

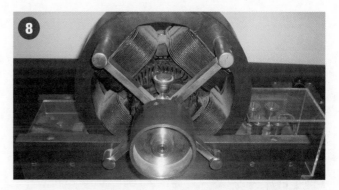

Tesla....came up with alternating current (AC) transmission. Instead of electricity going in one direction, it would move rapidly back and forth. This would allow it to carry higher levels of electricity more efficiently over long distances than DC transmission. He...built a small ...AC motor.

10. ThinkSpeakListen

Compare and contrast Tesla and Edison as inventors.

George Westinghouse

A businessman named George Westinghouse saw AC's potential and bought Tesla's patent in 1885....

Edison tried to persuade people that AC current was too dangerous....

Tesla argued that DC current was too weak and inefficient.

....Edison and Westinghouse, using Tesla's ideas, competed...to provide electricity for the lights of the Chicago World's Fair in 1893.... The two sides set up rival systems. But when they were turned on, Edison's lights looked dim compared with Tesla's. AC power won the battle.

From 1893 to 1896, he worked on a...project to harness the power of Niagara Falls for electricity.... When a switch was flipped on, electricity flowed to the city of Buffalo, miles away. Tesla...created the first successful hydroelectric project.

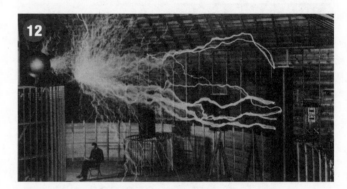

In 1891, Tesla invented the Tesla coil. This device uses electricity from devices such as radios and televisions. It then transforms it into very high voltage.... Larger Tesla coils can emit, or produce, bolts of lightning and sparks of electricity.

11. ThinkSpeakListen

Talk about Tesla and Edison. Do you think one was a better scientist than the other? Why?

Expand Sentences with Prepositional Phrases

Scientists call Tesla "the father of the electric age" **for** his revolutionary inventions.

He did not focus his energies on science **until** he prepared to come to the United States at the age of twenty-eight.

One reason for this was because Tesla competed **throughout** his career with fellow inventor Thomas Edison.

But **after** Tesla presented his improvements to Edison, Edison said that he had been joking about the $50,000.

Edison had developed direct current (DC) transmission—a way of sending electricity **over** long distances.

12. ThinkSpeakListen

Describe one of Tesla's or Edison's inventions.

A Night in Tesla's Lab

Last night I dreamed that I visited Nikola Tesla in his laboratory. Why did I dream of this great scientist and inventor? Maybe it's because I'm reading about Tesla in school, or maybe it's because his inventions fascinate me!

In my dream, Tesla and I were friends. As we talked in his lab, Tesla.... described how he had emigrated from Europe to America with just four cents in his pocket....

He demonstrated a coil that he had invented, and I audibly gasped as the coil generated a spectacular electrical display. Next Tesla showed me his early X-ray shadowgraphs and a radio-controlled boat that he had built.... I was about to ask Tesla more when I heard a voice.

"Chris, it's time to get up!" Dad was shaking my shoulder.

"What a dream," I said as I sat up in bed. "I spent the entire night in Tesla's laboratory and I didn't even get his autograph!"

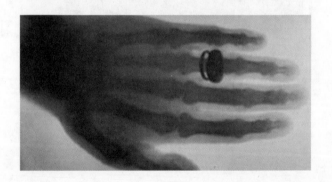

13. ThinkSpeakListen

Describe details of the narrator's dream about Tesla's laboratory.

Research and Writing

Informative/Explanatory

<u>Research one invention or discovery that has affected the way we power our lives.</u> <u>In an opinion essay, explain why you think this invention or discovery has had the greatest impact on the way we use electricity.</u> <u>Make sure to defend your opinion with reasons and evidence.</u>

Research you will do

Essay you will write

Evidence you will use

Sample Essay

In today's world, people do not want to rely on electrical outlets. How could we use our computers as we travel? How could we talk on our cell phones wherever we are? The reason we are able to use technology on the go is the existence of the battery, first invented in 1800 by a man named Alesandro Volta. By making mobile technology possible, the battery is the invention that has had the greatest impact on how we power our lives today.

The writer introduces the topic and states an opinion.

One way in which we depend on batteries is in our ability to communicate on the go. According to the Society for Communications Research, over 50 percent of all Americans report that they use a cell phone at least once per day. Without batteries to power these phones, the lives of millions of people would be very different.

Another form of technology that would not be possible without batteries is the portable computer. "Portable computers have changed the way that millions of people do their jobs, by allowing them to take their work wherever they go," explains Amelia Thomas, a social science professor at the Tampa Institute of Technology. Without batteries, employees all over the world would be much less productive, since they could not do as much work while traveling.

The writer supports his/her opinion with reasons and source evidence.

Volta's battery is the invention that has had the greatest impact on how we use technology today. In fact, some say that there would be no "modern technology" without Volta's discovery. It is hard to imagine how the cell phones and other mobile devices we rely on every day would even exist. No wonder the "volt" is named after him!

The writer restates the opinion and makes a concluding statement.

Common Core State Standards

CA CCSS Reading Standards for Literature

RL.4.1	Refer to details and examples in a text when explaining what the text says explicitly and when drawing inferences from the text.
RL.4.2	Determine a theme of a story, drama, or poem from details in the text; summarize the text.
RL.4.3	Describe in depth a character, setting, or event in a story or drama, drawing on specific details in the text (e.g., a character's thoughts, words, or actions).
RL.4.4	Determine the meaning of words and phrases as they are used in a text, including those that allude to significant characters found in mythology (e.g., Herculean). **(See grade 4 Language standards 4–6 for additional expectations.) CA**
RL.4.5	Explain major differences between poems, drama, and prose, and refer to the structural elements of poems (e.g., verse, rhythm, meter) and drama (e.g., casts of characters, settings, descriptions, dialogue, stage directions) when writing or speaking about a text.
RL.4.6	Compare and contrast the point of view from which different stories are narrated, including the difference between first- and third-person narrations.
RL.4.7	Make connections between the text of a story or drama and a visual or oral presentation of the text, identifying where each version reflects specific descriptions and directions in the text.
RL.4.9	Compare and contrast the treatment of similar themes and topics (e.g., opposition of good and evil) and patterns of events (e.g., the quest) in stories, myths, and traditional literature from different cultures.
RL.4.10	By the end of the year, read and comprehend literature, including stories, dramas, and poetry, in the grades 4–5 text complexity band proficiently, with scaffolding as needed at the high end of the range.

CA CCSS Reading Standards for Informational Text

RI.4.1	Refer to details and examples in a text when explaining what the text says explicitly and when drawing inferences from the text.
RI.4.2	Determine the main idea of a text and explain how it is supported by key details; summarize the text.
RI.4.3	Explain events, procedures, ideas, or concepts in a historical, scientific, or technical text, including what happened and why, based on specific information in the text.
RI.4.4	Determine the meaning of general academic and domain-specific words or phrases in a text relevant to a *grade 4 topic or subject area*. **(See grade 4 Language standards 4–6 for additional expectations.) CA**
RI.4.5	Describe the overall structure (e.g., chronology, comparison, cause/effect, problem/solution) of events, ideas, concepts, or information in a text or part of a text.
RI.4.6	Compare and contrast a firsthand and secondhand account of the same event or topic; describe the differences in focus and the information provided.
RI.4.7	Interpret information presented visually, orally, or quantitatively (e.g., in charts, graphs, diagrams, time lines, animations, or interactive elements on Web pages) and explain how the information contributes to an understanding of the text in which it appears.
RI.4.8	Explain how an author uses reasons and evidence to support particular points in a text.
RI.4.9	Integrate information from two texts on the same topic in order to write or speak about the subject knowledgeably.
RI.4.10	By the end of year, read and comprehend informational texts, including history/social studies, science, and technical texts, in the grades 4–5 text complexity band proficiently, with scaffolding as needed at the high end of the range.

CA CCSS Reading Standards for Foundational Skills

RF.4.3	Know and apply grade-level phonics and word analysis skills in decoding words. a. Use combined knowledge of all letter-sound correspondences, syllabication patterns, and morphology (e.g., roots and affixes) to read accurately unfamiliar multisyllabic words in context and out of context.
RF.4.4	Read with sufficient accuracy and fluency to support comprehension. a. Read grade-level text with purpose and understanding. b. Read grade-level prose and poetry orally with accuracy, appropriate rate, and expression on successive readings. c. Use context to confirm or self-correct word recognition and understanding, rereading as necessary.

CA CCSS Writing Standards

W.4.1	Write opinion pieces on topics or texts, supporting a point of view with reasons and information. a. Introduce a topic or text clearly, state an opinion, and create an organizational structure in which related ideas are grouped to support the writer's purpose. b. Provide reasons that are supported by facts and details. c. Link opinion and reasons using words and phrases (e.g., *for instance, in order to, in addition*). d. Provide a concluding statement or section related to the opinion presented.
W.4.2	Write informative/explanatory texts to examine a topic and convey ideas and information clearly. a. Introduce a topic clearly and group related information in paragraphs and sections; include formatting (e.g., headings), illustrations, and multimedia when useful to aiding comprehension. b. Develop the topic with facts, definitions, concrete details, quotations, or other information and examples related to the topic. c. Link ideas within categories of information using words and phrases (e.g., *another, for example, also, because*). d. Use precise language and domain-specific vocabulary to inform about or explain the topic. e. Provide a concluding statement or section related to the information or explanation presented.
W.4.3	Write narratives to develop real or imagined experiences or events using effective technique, descriptive details, and clear event sequences. a. Orient the reader by establishing a situation and introducing a narrator and/or characters; organize an event sequence that unfolds naturally. b. Use dialogue and description to develop experiences and events or show the responses of characters to situations. c. Use a variety of transitional words and phrases to manage the sequence of events. d. Use concrete words and phrases and sensory details to convey experiences and events precisely. e. Provide a conclusion that follows from the narrated experiences or events.
W.4.4	Produce clear and coherent writing **(including multiple–paragraph texts)** in which the development and organization are appropriate to task, purpose, and audience. (Grade-specific expectations for writing types are defined in standards 1–3 above.) **CA**
W.4.5	With guidance and support from peers and adults, develop and strengthen writing as needed by planning, revising, and editing. (Editing for conventions should demonstrate command of Language standards 1–3 up to and including grade 4.)
W.4.6	With some guidance and support from adults, use technology, including the Internet, to produce and publish writing as well as to interact and collaborate with others; demonstrate sufficient command of keyboarding skills to type a minimum of one page in a single sitting.
W.4.7	Conduct short research projects that build knowledge through investigation of different aspects of a topic.
W.4.8	Recall relevant information from experiences or gather relevant information from print and digital sources; take notes, **paraphrase,** and categorize information, and provide a list of sources. **CA**
W.4.9	Draw evidence from literary or informational texts to support analysis, reflection, and research. a. Apply *grade 4 Reading standards* to literature (e.g., "Describe in depth a character, setting, or event in a story or drama, drawing on specific details in the text [e.g., a character's thoughts, words, or actions]."). b. Apply *grade 4 Reading standards* to informational texts (e.g., "Explain how an author uses reasons and evidence to support particular points in a text").
W.4.10	Write routinely over extended time frames (time for research, reflection, and revision) and shorter time frames (a single sitting or a day or two) for a range of discipline-specific tasks, purposes, and audiences.

CA CCSS Speaking and Listening Standards

SL.4.1	Engage effectively in a range of collaborative discussions (one-on-one, in groups, and teacher-led) with diverse partners on grade 4 topics and texts, building on others' ideas and expressing their own clearly. a. Come to discussions prepared, having read or studied required material; explicitly draw on that preparation and other information known about the topic to explore ideas under discussion. b. Follow agreed-upon rules for discussions and carry out assigned roles. c. Pose and respond to specific questions to clarify or follow up on information, and make comments that contribute to the discussion and link to the remarks of others. d. Review the key ideas expressed and explain their own ideas and understanding in light of the discussion.
SL.4.2	Paraphrase portions of a text read aloud or information presented in diverse media and formats, including visually, quantitatively, and orally.
SL.4.3	Identify the reasons and evidence a speaker **or media source** provides to support particular points. **CA**
SL.4.4	Report on a topic or text, tell a story, or recount an experience in an organized manner, using appropriate facts and relevant, descriptive details to support main ideas or themes; speak clearly at an understandable pace. **a. Plan and deliver a narrative presentation that: relates ideas, observations, or recollections; provides a clear context; and includes clear insight into why the event or experience is memorable. CA**
SL.4.5	Add audio recordings and visual displays to presentations when appropriate to enhance the development of main ideas or themes.
SL.4.6	Differentiate between contexts that call for formal English (e.g., presenting ideas) and situations where informal discourse is appropriate (e.g., small-group discussion); use formal English when appropriate to task and situation. (See grade 4 Language standards 1 and 3 for specific expectations.)

CA CCSS Language Standards

L.4.1	Demonstrate command of the conventions of standard English grammar and usage when writing or speaking. a. Use **interrogative**, relative pronouns (*who, whose, whom, which, that*) and relative adverbs (*where, when, why*). **CA** b. Form and use the progressive (e.g., *I was walking; I am walking; I will be walking*) verb tenses. c. Use modal auxiliaries (e.g., *can, may, must*) to convey various conditions. d. Order adjectives within sentences according to conventional patterns (e.g., *a small red bag* rather than *a red small bag*). e. Form and use prepositional phrases. f. Produce complete sentences, recognizing and correcting inappropriate fragments and run-ons. g. Correctly use frequently confused words (e.g., *to, too, two; there, their*). **h. Write fluidly and legibly in cursive or joined italics. CA**
L.4.2	Demonstrate command of the conventions of standard English capitalization, punctuation, and spelling when writing: a. Use correct capitalization. b. Use commas and quotation marks to mark direct speech and quotations from a text. c. Use a comma before a coordinating conjunction in a compound sentence. d. Spell grade-appropriate words correctly, consulting references as needed.
L.4.3	Use knowledge of language and its conventions when writing, speaking, reading, or listening. a. Choose words and phrases to convey ideas precisely. b. Choose punctuation for effect. c. Differentiate between contexts that call for formal English (e.g., presenting ideas) and situations where informal discourse is appropriate (e.g., small-group discussion).
L.4.4	Determine or clarify the meaning of unknown and multiple-meaning words and phrases based on *grade 4 reading and content*, choosing flexibly from a range of strategies. a. Use context (e.g., definitions, examples, or restatements in text) as a clue to the meaning of a word or phrase. b. Use common, grade-appropriate Greek and Latin affixes and roots as clues to the meaning of a word (e.g., *telegraph, photograph, autograph*). c. Consult reference materials (e.g., dictionaries, glossaries, thesauruses), both print and digital, to find the pronunciation and determine or clarify the precise meaning of key words and phrases **and to identify alternate word choices in all content areas. CA**
L.4.5	Demonstrate understanding of figurative language, word relationships, and nuances in word meanings. a. Explain the meaning of simple similes and metaphors (e.g., as pretty as a picture) in context. b. Recognize and explain the meaning of common idioms, adages, and proverbs. c. Demonstrate understanding of words by relating them to their opposites (antonyms) and to words with similar but not identical meanings (synonyms).
L.4.6	Acquire and use accurately grade-appropriate general academic and domain-specific words and phrases, including those that signal precise actions, emotions, or states of being (e.g., *quizzed, whined, stammered*) and that are basic to a particular topic (e.g., *wildlife, conservation*, and *endangered* when discussing animal preservation).

California English Language Development Standards

CA ELD Part I: Interacting in Meaningful Ways

ELD.PI.4.1	Exchanging information and ideas with others through oral collaborative conversations on a range of social and academic topics
ELD.PI.4.2	Interacting with others in written English in various communicative forms (print, communicative technology, and multimedia)
ELD.PI.4.3	Offering and supporting opinions and negotiating with others in communicative exchanges
ELD.PI.4.4	Adapting language choices to various contexts (based on task, purpose, audience, and text type)
ELD.PI.4.5	Listening actively to spoken English in a range of social and academic contexts
ELD.PI.4.6	Reading closely literary and informational texts and viewing multimedia to determine how meaning is conveyed explicitly and implicitly through language
ELD.PI.4.7	Evaluating how well writers and speakers use language to support ideas and opinions with details or reasons depending on modality, text type, purpose, audience, topic, and content area
ELD.PI.4.8	Analyzing how writers and speakers use vocabulary and other language resources for specific purposes (to explain, persuade, entertain, etc.) depending on modality, text type, purpose, audience, topic, and content area
ELD.PI.4.9	Expressing information and ideas in formal oral presentations on academic topics
ELD.PI.4.10	Writing literary and informational texts to present, describe, and explain ideas and information, using appropriate technology
ELD.PI.4.11	Supporting own opinions and evaluating others' opinions in speaking and writing
ELD.PI.4.12	Selecting and applying varied and precise vocabulary and other language resources to effectively convey ideas

CA ELD Part II: Learning About How English Works

ELD.PII.4.1	Understanding text structure
ELD.PII.4.2	Understanding cohesion
ELD.PII.4.3	Using verbs and verb phrases
ELD.PII.4.4	Using nouns and noun phrases
ELD.PII.4.5	Modifying to add details
ELD.PII.4.6	Connecting ideas
ELD.PII.4.7	Condensing ideas

CA ELD Part III: Using Foundational Literacy Skills

ELD.PIII.4.1	See Appendix A [in *Foundational Literacy Skills for English Learners*] for information on teaching reading foundational skills to English learners of various profiles based on age, native language, native language writing system, schooling experience, and literacy experience and proficiency. Some considerations are: • Native language and literacy (e.g., phoneme awareness or print concept skills in native language) should be assessed for potential transference to English language and literacy. • Similarities between native language and English should be highlighted (e.g., phonemes or letters that are the same in both languages). • Differences between native language and English should be highlighted (e.g., some phonemes in English may not exist in the student's native language; native language syntax may be different from English syntax).

Benchmark ADVANCE
Texts for English Language Development

Credits
Editors: Gregory Blume, Joanne Tangorra
Creative Director: Laurie Berger
Art Directors: Christina Cirillo, Doug McGredy
Production: Kosta Triantafillis
Director of Photography: Doug Schneider
Photo Assistant: Jackie Friedman

Photo credits: Cover D: © nik wheeler / Alamy; Title Page B: © Richard Eaton / Demotix/Demotix/Demotix/Corbis; Title Page C: CHUCK KENNEDY/KRT/Newscom; Page 4D: LIZ ROLL/UPI/Newscom; Page 5A: Splash News/Newscom; Page 8B: Granger, NYC; Page 10A: Nagel Photography / Shutterstock.com; Page 10B: REUTERS/Robert Galbraith; Page 10C, 12A, 12D: ASSOCIATED PRESS; Page 12B: a katz / Shutterstock.com; Page 13: MICHAEL NELSON/EPA/Newscom; Page 15B: JOE BURBANK / POOL/EPA/Newscom; Page 19C: © Todd Bannor / Alamy; Page 22: © AF archive / Alamy; Page 24a, 24b, 25: The Lion and the Gnat (chromolitho), French School, (19th century) / Private Collection / © Look and Learn / Bridgeman Images; Page 34b, 34c: Granger, NYC; Page 40a, 41a: Mary Evans Pictures Library; Page 40b: © The Protected Art Archive / Alamy; Page 40c: © PARIS PIERCE / Alamy; Page 41b: MGM / THE KOBAL COLLECTION; Page 42: © Bettmann/CORBIS; Page 44C: © Jana Thompson / Alamy; Page 46A: akg-images/Newscom; Page 48C: © Michael Pearcy / Alamy; Page 51B: © Lightwriter1949; Page 54c: © Rabbitrabbit002 | Dreamstime.com - Groundhog Day, Raleigh Photo; Page 56a: Everett Collection/Newscom; Page 57c: © C.O. Mercial / Alamy; Page 58A: Granger, NYC; Page 60b: © North Wind Picture Archives; Page 74C: © Bettmann/CORBIS; Page 83a: © Kristin Piljay / Alamy; Page 83b: © Kristoffer Tripplaar / Alamy; Page 84a: © Jeff Greenberg / Alamy; Page 91b, 100b: ASSOCIATED PRESS; Page 92a: © WorldFoto / Alamy; Page 94a: © Hollandse Hoogte/Corbis; Page 94b: © Idealink Photography / Alamy; Page 95a: Olga Besnard / Shutterstock.com; Page 95b, 96a: NIC BOTHMA/EPA/Newscom; Page 95d, 98d: © Dasha Rosato / Alamy; Page 96b: Eric Broder Van Dyke/Shutterstock.com; Page 96c, 98a: © Jim West / Alamy; Page 96d: Dong liu / Shutterstock.com; Page 97a: © Frances Roberts / Alamy; PagePage 98b: © JIM LO SCALZO/epa/Corbis; Page 122: Crossing the Ford, Platte River, Colorado (oil on canvas), Whittredge, Thomas Worthington (1820-1910) / Century Association, New York, USA / Bridgeman Images; Page 123A, 124A, 125A, 126A, 126D, 127A, 127C, 128B, 128C, 130B, 130C, 133A, 133D, 136C, 137C, 138B, 138D, 141: Granger, NYC; Page 124B: Black 1914 Model T Ford (USA), side view, . / Dorling Kindersley/UIG / Bridgeman Images; Page 124D, 125C, 126C, 130A, 130D, 131B, 138C, 140C: Library of Congress; Page 125B: © Vintage Images / Alamy; Page 127D: © Pictorial Press Ltd / Alamy; Page 131D, 134C, 141B: © North Wind Picture Archives / Alamy; Page 131E: Railroad Construction Crew, 1886 (b/w photo), American Photographer, (19th century) / Private Collection / Peter Newark American Pictures / Bridgeman Images; Page 132A: © GraphicaArtis/Corbis; Page 132B: © Niday Picture Library / Alamy; Page 132C: Train Passengers on the Kansas Pacific Railroad, shooting buffalo for sport in the 1870's (colour litho), American School, (19th century) / Private Collection / Peter Newark Western Americana / Bridgeman Images; Page 133B: © Stephen Saks Photography / Alamy; Page 134B: © Mary Evans Picture Library / Alamy; Page 136A: © North Wind Picture Archives -- All rights reserved; Page 136B: "Lewis and Clark at Three Forks" by Edgar S. Paxon, Oil on Canvas, 1912, Montana Historical Society, Montana State Capitol Art Collection, X1912.07.01, Don Beatty Photographer 10/1999; Page 137A: © ClassicStock / Alamy; Page 137B: Whitman Mission National Historic Site; Page 137D: © Corbis; Page 138A: Joan Helm Jensen Collection/Oregon Historical Society/#bb011799; Page 139A, 139B, 139C: © Paul John Fearn / Alamy; Page 140A: © Dennis Frates / Alamy; Page 140B: © PARIS PIERCE / Alamy; Page 142: © Manpreet Romana/Getty Images; Page 143a: © MARK COSTANTINI/San Francisco Chronicle/corbis; Page 145b: James P. Blair / Contributor / Getty Images; Page 148b: JIJI PRESS / Stringer / Getty Images; Page 148c: The Asahi Shimbun / Contributor / Getty Images; Page 152c: © Stock Italia / Alamy; Page 152d: © Aflo/Corbis; Page 153e: Hill Street Studios/Getty Images; Page 154c: John T. Barr / Contributor / Getty Images; Page 162, 176a: © RGB Ventures / SuperStock / Alamy; Page 163a: Universal Images Group; Page 164a, 171a, 174b: Library of Congress; Page 164d, 168b, 170b, 170c, 171b, 171c, 171d: Granger, NYC; Page 165: © Curt Teich Postcard A; Page 166a: © Ted Streshinsky/CORBIS; Page 166b: © Ted Soqui/Corbis; Page 168a: ASSOCIATED PRESS; Page 168c: © Bettmann/CORBIS; Page 170a, 177, 178b: © Corbis; Page 170d: © ClassicStock / Alamy; Page 172b: Michael Rougier; Page 172c: © L.M. OTERO/AP/Corbis; Page 172d: © Richard Hamilton Smith/CORBIS; Page 175a: © North Wind Picture Archives / Alamy; Page 175c: © 19th era 2 / Alamy; Page 179b: © Gari Wyn Williams / Alamy; Page 180a, 180b: Library of Congress; The Crowley; Page 183b: Detlev van Ravensway / Science Source; Page 184c: © Bikas Das/ /AP/Corbis; Page 185: REUTERS GRAPHICS; Page 186b: Artist's impression of the Benjamin Franklin's / Universal History Archive/UIG / Bridgeman Images; Page 187c: Library of Congress; Page 188b, 188c: © Bettmann/CORBIS; Page 192b: BOB GOMEL / Page 192c: DETLEV VAN RAVENSWAAY/SCIENCE PHOTO LIBRARY; Page 193: © nobleIMAGES / Alamy; Page 196b, 199b: © Niday Picture Library / Alamy; Page 200b: Peter Menzel / Science Source

Art credits: Pages 26-27, 29: Ghyslaine Vaysset; Page 28: Christina Cirillo; Page 80: Loren E. Mack; 146-147, 149, 156-160: Joel Spector

Permissions: "The First Town Meeting" from *The People Of Sparks: The Second Book Of Ember* by Jeanne DuPrau, copyright © 2004 by Jeanne DuPrau. Used by permission of Random House Children's Books, a division of Random House LLC. All rights reserved.

Excerpt from *Holes* © 1998 by Louis Sachar. Reprinted by permission of Farrar, Straus, and Giroux, LLC. All Rights Reserved.

Excerpt from *Stormy, Misty's Foal* by Marguerite Henry reprinted with the permission of Aladdin Paperbacks, an imprint of Simon & Schuster Children's Publishing Division. Copyright © 1963 Macmillan Publishing Company.

Excerpt from *Because of Winn-Dixie*, copyright © 2000 by Kate DiCamillo. Reproduced by permission of the publisher Candlewick Press, Inc., Somerville, MA.

Dust Bowl Refugee words and music by Woody Guthrie WGP/TRO,© copyright 1960 (Renewed), 1963 (Renewed) Woody Guthrie Publications, Inc. & Ludlow Music, Inc., New York, NY administered by Ludlow Music, Inc. Used by permission.

Excerpt from *Cesar: Si, se puede!/Yes, We Can* copyright © 2004 by Carmen T. Bernier-Grand, illustrated by David Diaz, reprinted by permissions of Amazon Publishing, Inc.

Excerpt from *Out of the Dust* by Karen Hesse. Copyright © 1997 by Karen Hesse. Reprinted by permission of Scholastic Inc.

"Power Restored in India" from *TIME for Kids*, August 1, 2012. © 2012 Time Inc. All rights reserved.

ISBN: 978-1-5021-6646-3